THE HERITAGE HANDBOOK

An A-Z guide to the archaeology and landscape history of Northern Devon

Published by:
Museum of Barnstaple and North Devon

ISBN 978-0-9933596-0-6

Published with the aid of:
The Barnstaple Bridge Trust,
The Bideford Bridge Trust
Fullabrook Community Interest Fund
Lyn Financial Services
South West Archaeology Ltd

Design: Bruce Aiken

Front cover:
Remnants of a fish weir on the Taw Estuary at Ashford

THE HERITAGE HANDBOOK

An A-Z guide to the archaeology and landscape history of Northern Devon

Compiled by
John Bradbeer and Terry Green
For the North Devon Archaeological Society

With contributions from
Richard Bass
Derry Bryant
Peter Claughton
David Dawson
Paul Madgett
Chris Preece
Martin Watts

Foreword

The stated objective of the North Devon Archaeological Society is to 'promote awareness of the archaeology and history of North Devon'. With this in view, we have compiled this collection of brief (some not so brief) articles on aspects and features of the area which, in our view, contribute to an in depth understanding of the evolution of the Northern Devon landscape and the communities within it. The articles presented here represent the current state of knowledge, most of it to be found in the existing literature, parts of it contributed by specialists specifically for our purpose, but brought together here in, we hope, an easily accessible and convenient form – a handbook for the curious, in fact. We hope that there will be interest here for local residents, for newcomers to the area and for seasonal visitors.

Note that we are providing an overview of the archaeology and landscape history of *Northern* Devon. We have defined Northern Devon as being the two modern local government areas of North Devon and Torridge, although we have allowed ourselves to make mention in passing of a few places further afield, in particular on the Somerset side of Exmoor and across the border in north-east Cornwall, which has more in common with Northern Devon than it does with the rest of Cornwall beyond Tintagel. Where we have found it necessary to place our topics in a broader context, we have of course strayed beyond our borders to other parts of the South West or even farther afield. We have chosen an alphabetic 'A-Z' format in order to emphasise that this book is meant, as much as anything, to be a guide, either to be browsed at home or to be at hand on walks or car journeys. We have, as far as possible, cited - with national grid references - examples of sites which can be viewed from publicly accessible land, perhaps a road or a public footpath. (See Appendix B for help with reading a National Grid reference.)

We must emphasise here that it is never permissible to enter private land without the permission of the landowner. Possession of this guide does not in any way imply permission.

Northern Devon tends to present something of a blank on distribution maps of archaeological sites. There are a variety of historic reasons for this, but the end result is an impression that somehow the area has been bypassed by history. This is patently not true, since our entire landscape has been shaped by human activity over thousands of years. The more likely reason is that the attention of archaeologists has been directed elsewhere, and so the evidence has not been brought to light. However, as is commonly restated among archaeologists, absence of evidence is not evidence of absence; we hope therefore that this brief guide to what we know about Northern Devon will stimulate interest and lead some among its readers to indulge their curiosity and find out more.

North Devon Archaeological Society wishes to thank The Barnstaple Bridge Trust, The Bideford Bridge Trust, Fullabrook Community Interest Fund, Lyn Financial Services Ltd and South West Archaeology Ltd for their sponsorship of this work, Bruce Aiken for his work on the graphic design and Linda Blanchard, Robert Higham and Alison Mills for their comments on the draft text.

Location map showing places mentioned in the text

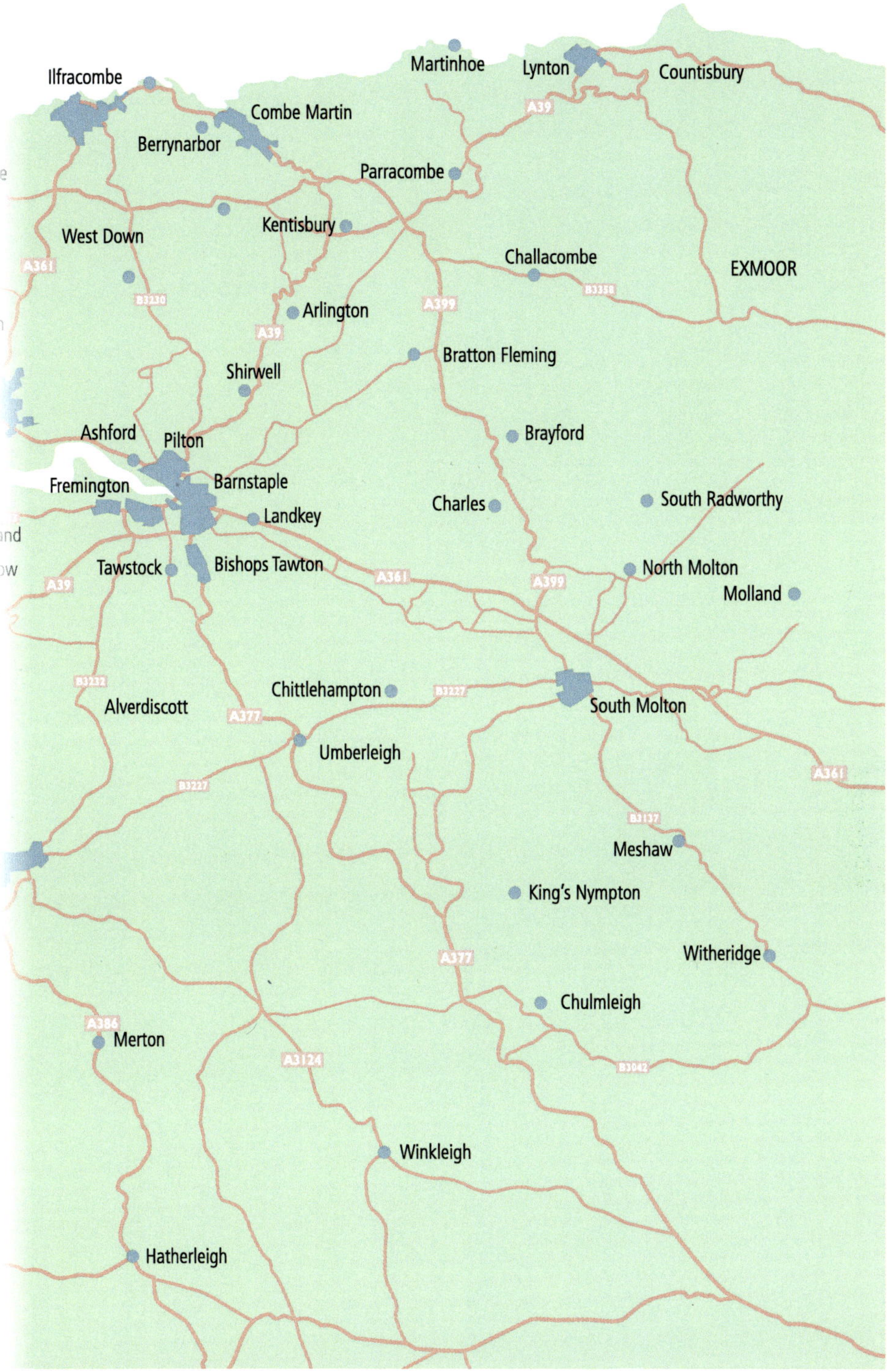

Ilfracombe
Martinhoe
Lynton
Countisbury
Combe Martin
Berrynarbor
A39
Parracombe
West Down
Kentisbury
A361
Challacombe
EXMOOR
B3230
Arlington
A399
B3358
A39
Bratton Fleming
Shirwell
Brayford
Ashford
Pilton
Barnstaple
Fremington
Landkey
Charles
South Radworthy
Tawstock
Bishops Tawton
A39
A361
A399
North Molton
Molland
B3232
Chittlehampton
B3227
South Molton
Alverdiscott
A377
Umberleigh
A361
B3227
B3137
Meshaw
King's Nympton
Witheridge
A377
Chulmleigh
A386
Merton
A3124
B3042
Winkleigh
Hatherleigh

Introduction

Archaeology may be roughly defined as the study of human activity in the past through artefacts, environmental traces, human remains and cultural landscapes. Artefacts include those handed down the generations, those deliberately buried and those discarded as unwanted rubbish or perhaps simply lost, while cultural landscapes include earthworks, standing buildings, settlements, field-systems, trackways and the linguistic traces found in place-names. Environmental traces are among the most recently appreciated evidence and include both plant material and insect remains most frequently preserved in anaerobic wet conditions. All of these strands of evidence complement each other and the task of the archaeologist is to integrate the evidence in order to reconstruct the lives and world of our ancestors. It might be thought that a number of entries in this gazetteer are more 'historical' than 'archaeological', but this is an unsafe distinction. Our knowledge of the past draws on a broad spectrum of evidence from the purely physical (archaeology) to the purely documentary (history). In between these extremes the physical remains of human activity provide information where documents are lacking and serve to augment – or even contradict – documentary evidence, while at the same time written histories help us to make sense of what we find buried or what see around us. Accepting therefore that all matter that comes down to us from the past – from Mesolithic flint work to 19th century railway viaducts or even physical remnants of the 20th century Cold War – is evidence in the archaeological sense, this handbook outlines some of what is known about the archaeology of Northern Devon, with a particular focus on the artefacts, the components of the cultural landscape and the historical movements that have contributed to their development. It is not primarily a gazetteer of archaeological sites, although most of the classic sites find a place somewhere among the entries, but rather a handy reference work for the curious. The A-Z element is slightly wishful thinking, for it is not possible to find a suitable entry for all the letters of the alphabet but we trust that most topics that our readers would hope to find are indeed covered.

Archaeology grew out of what the 19th century called antiquarian interest and even into the twentieth century, many of the earlier archaeological discoveries in Northern Devon and elsewhere were made by enthusiastic amateurs. Although techniques of digging, recording and interpretation became well developed during the early 20th century, the results of this early work tantalise as much as they inform. With a heavy emphasis on artefacts or 'bones and stones', lacking any absolute dating method (radio-carbon dating was only developed in the 1950s) and ignoring any organic evidence, the early archaeologists had difficulty forming a reliable picture of the past with real people leading real lives. Today things are very different. On the one hand, there is the academic input of university departments and on the other, the work of professional commercial archaeological units investigating ahead of development, as, in principle, required by the planning process; in addition there is the input of national bodies such as English Heritage and Historic England, regional bodies such as the National Parks and county –based heritage services as well as of local archaeological societies and of well informed individual enthusiasts. Through the use of increasingly sophisticated modern techniques both in the field and in the laboratory, our understanding of the past, including that of Northern Devon, is being enhanced and refined.

Much of the area covered by this book formed the core of Grinsell's 1970 book, *The Archaeology of Exmoor: Bideford Bay to Bridgwater*, which remains the most complete account of

Northern Devon's archaeology. The Exmoor National Park, which includes a part of north-east Devon, has been subject to a further more recent survey by Hazel Riley and Rob Wilson-North, published by English Heritage as The Field Archaeology of Exmoor and this present book draws on its scholarship. Other general and subject specific works are listed at the end of the book as well as in the 'Further Reading' appended to each entry.It will be noted that the area to the south and west of Bideford has received far less attention than the eastern part of our area and it is to be hoped that this shortcoming will be rectified in time.

Axes: stone and bronze

The earliest evidence of an axe that we have in Britain dates from the Mesolithic period, roughly 10,000 to 6,000 years ago, when hunter-gatherers moved into post-glacial Britain in pursuit of forest game. The Mesolithic axe was a crude affair, a flint or chert core shaped to be set into a haft and with an edge achieved through simple knapping. Applied to timber of small diameter, it chewed through the wood rather than really cutting. Nevertheless it is probable that inroads were made into the woodland, perhaps principally in order to create clearings where fresh grass would attract game.

Neolithic greenstone axes.

The arrival of the first farmers in Britain signalled the beginning of the period that we call the Neolithic or 'new stone age'. In this context the name has particular significance, since the characteristic Neolithic axe is a very different product. Carefully shaped to a trapezoidal form, the flint or chert was then laboroiusly ground and polished producing a smooth implement with a sharp edge. This was a much improved tool designed to despatch trees of any dimension and with it forest clearance began, creating land for growing crops. Possibly owing to its ability to transform forest into productive land, the polished stone axe appears to have acquired symbolic significance, so that what are taken to be ritual deposits of polished stone axes are known from Britain and Scandinavia. It is probable that they were also the subject of formal gift exchange between tribal groups which may explain the examples that are known from Northern Devon. We have as yet hardly any examples of functional polished flint axes in the area – which is not to say that more did not exist; on the other hand we do have a number of axe-like objects of polished 'greenstone', a volcanic rock outcropping in the Lake District, Scotland and Cornwall. These stone 'axes', which mimic the shape of polished flint axes, do not appear to be functional - unless they were used as battle-axes rather than for cutting wood - and appear to be made for ritual gift exchange, their distance from the geological source suggesting an elaborate trade or exchange network embracing the whole of Britain.

Very different are the first metal axes. Copper began to be smelted in southern Europe around 7,000BC and to be fashioned into blades including axes which appear to be entirely functional. The discovery that the addition of tin to copper produced a harder metal transformed copper technology into a

Bronze Age axe-heads from Northern Devon.

bronze technology characterising the cultural period that we know as the Bronze Age. Among the items of bronze produced at this time were so-called flat axes, which were presumably set into a haft in the same way as a stone axe. Over time the design improved, mostly in the direction of better ways of fixing the axe-head to the haft. Thus we find examples with a socket, others with flanges and yet others with a loop through which to pass, perhaps, a thong. In older publications these are often referred to as 'celts' or 'palstaves'. Examples of all these types turn up occasionally in Northern Devon, through the activities of metal detectorists. (TG)

Further Reading:
No specific title, but an Internet search will locate lot of information. Typing in *Images for prehistoric axes in Britain and Ireland* brings up a broad spectrum of axes from the Palaeolithic to the early Middle Ages.

Barrows

What we call 'barrows' (from Old English beorg 'mound, hill') are prehistoric burial mounds, ie. soil mounded over a burial place. Burial, in a prehistoric context may have involved interment of the whole body or the depositing of cremated remains. Archaeologists recognise two principal types of barrow: long barrows and round barrows. Long barrows are typical of the Neolithic period (4000 – 2500 BC). In these the long, earthen mound may cover a series of stone-built chambers containing the bones of the dead. They seem to represent a practice of communal burial. There are no clear examples of long barrows in our area, but are typically found farther east on the Wessex chalk lands and in the Cotswolds.

Round barrows are more typical of the late Neolithic to Middle Bronze Age period, roughly 2500 to 1500 BC and are quite frequently to be seen in Northern Devon and Exmoor.

The highest of the Chapman Barrows marking the parish boundary between Parracombe and Challacombe.

Typically a round barrow is a circular earthen mound perhaps surrounded by a ditch or a stone kerb. In most cases that have been investigated the mound covers a single central burial represented by either cremated bone contained within an urn or a skeleton. There may also be secondary burials inserted into the earth of the mound. Round barrows frequently occur in groups known as barrow cemeteries. In our area the most prominent and well preserved example is the group known as Chapman Barrows (SS69-43-) on west Exmoor where they define the boundary between the parishes of Parracombe and Challacombe. The location on a prominent high point is typical, as for example at Five Barrows near Brayford (SS73-36) where there are in fact nine, Berry Down (SS54-43-) near Berrynarbor and Martinhoe Common (SS67-48-). On Exmoor there are numerous well preserved examples, such as Wood Barrow (SS716 425), Long Stone Barrow (SS705 431) and Chains Barrow (SS735 419). Away from Exmoor, round barrows appear to be isolated, often standing as a single low mound in a field. In fact these may represent the isolated survivors of groups, the remainder of which have been ploughed flat over the centuries. Visible and accessible examples in the parish of East Putford are Bush Barrow at SS379 177, a barrow group nearby at Wrangworthy Cross SS385 174 and farther to the west on the boundary between Sutcombe and Pancrasweek parishes at SS341 095 is High Barrow. Aerial survey will often reveal the presence of lost barrows through crop or soil marks. Recent close examination of aerial survey records by the National Mapping Programme has revealed a number of previously unknown barrows and barrow groups, for example on Bursdon Moor, south of Hartland.

In Wessex, especially in Wiltshire and Dorset, round barrows appear in varied forms. In addition to the typical mound, known as a bowl barrow, we find disk barrows, bell barrows and pond barrows. What is probably a bell barrow can be seen beside the coast path above Gallantry Bower to the north-west of Clovelly (NGR: SS305 263).

Over the centuries the number of ancient barrows has been heavily reduced through the curiosity or the acquitive nature of later generations. Medieval kings were wont to grant licences to dig into barrows in search of treasure to help out the often cash-strapped Crown, while in the 18th and 19th centuries 'barrow digging' was a favourite pastime of local dignitaries with antiquarian interests. Guests might be entertained by watching a party of estate workmen digging into the centre of a barrow to recover the burial. This has led to the unfortunate fact that very great numbers of surviving round barrows have a depression in the centre where the barrow has been 'dug' without any of the meticulous care that modern archaeological practice would dictate. In some cases the spoils have been preserved in a museum, eg. the huge Berrynarbor urn to be seen in the RAMM in Exeter, but in most cases the artefacts and the information that they contained have been lost.

However, a discovery in the year 2011 – not actually in our area, though not far away – shows what we may have lost. The occasion was the excavation of a uniquely well preserved cist (stone box) burial within the peat on Whitehorse Hill, Dartmoor. This has been radio-carbon dated to around 2000 BC.

The astonishingly well preserved organic remains include a woven basket, nettle fibre textiles, leather work, expertly turned spindle wood ear studs, thread and a bracelet made of cow hair and an animal pelt (apparently bear) in which the cremated bone was wrapped, all together with a string of amber beads. This glimpse of the skillfully crafted stuff of everyday life brings to life Devon's Bronze Age in a so far unique way. (TG)

Further Reading:

Grinsell L V 1990: *Barrows in England and Wales*, Shire Publications.

Marsden B M 1999: *The Early Barrow Diggers,* Tempus Publishing, Stroud.

Bricks

Northern Devon did not have many structures built of brick until the nineteenth century. Local clays were valued for making pottery and tobacco pipes and, in the medieval period, ridge-tiles for roofs and patterned floor tiles rather than for bricks. One of the earliest securely dated brick-built houses in North Devon is to be seen at Number 28 Bridgeland Street, Bideford. Nathaniel Gascoyne's 'spec' for this handsome late 17th century house, dated 5th May 1693 and preserved in the North Devon Record Office, includes the requirement that the walls be 'built upwards with good brick and mortar'. This requirement echoed a growing fashion for the use of brick in 'polite' architecture. Other good examples of 17th/18th century brickwork are to be seen in Great Torrington at number 28 South Street and 83 New Street. The house in South Street may also be the work of Nathaniel Gascoyne. Early brick tends to be relatively thin and irregular, often with stone inclusions, though sizes have varied over time. Brick sizes were fixed by decree in 1571 at 9" x 4½" x 2¼"; such bricks were known as 'statute bricks'. In the later 18th century bricks became fatter because of the introduction

17th century brickwork on the corner of Holland Walk, Barnstaple.

Right: 18th/19th century 'hand made' brick. Far right: 19th century use of Marland brick at Bridge Chambers, Barnstaple, here laid in Flemish bond.

of a brick tax. These continued to be 'hand-made', and can be distinguished by their rough texture from the later regularly formed 'industrial' brick in use from the mid-19th century onwards. Where the early bricks were produced is not known, but the Summerland Street area of Barnstaple was developed in the 19th century on land that was known as the brickfields.

It was in the nineteenth century that brick production

became significant at Fremington and especially at Peters Marland, so that in most towns of Northern Devon nineteenth and early twentieth century houses and buildings are readily recognised, being at least faced with if not totally constructed from, the distinctive white or cream Marland bricks. (But note that in some cases, an earlier structure lies behind a Marland brick façade.) A variant on the use of brick in the 19th century is its employment to form the reveals of doors and windows in buildings – especially, but by no means exclusively agricultural buildings – which otherwise are of rubble-stone. Brick production at Peters Marland started on a large scale in 1878 and by 1901 the works was producing some 2.8 million bricks per annum. Production stopped in 1916 and resumed in 1925, again achieving an annual output of around 2 million bricks. The works closed in 1942, as the clay pit feeding the plant suffered from a major land-slip. The Marland works also produced drainage pipes and paving tiles. Fremington bricks were red in colour and many Victorian buildings employ both these and Marland white bricks to give patterns in the walls. The sites of brick-works at Fremington and Marland have been cleared and there is little evidence of their existence to be seen on the ground.

Far left: English bond. Near left: Flemish bond.

There are many distinctive styles of brickwork, depending on how each course of bricks is laid. Bricks laid long-ways are termed stretchers and those laid end-on are termed headers. When each course comprises alternating stretchers and headers, it is termed Flemish bond. Another common form of bonding is English bond, where courses alternate between those of stretchers and those of headers. A variant of this is double English bond, where two successive courses are headers, to be followed by a further two successive courses of stretchers. As a general rule English bond precedes Flemish bond, but this is not hard and fast. (JB)

Further reading:

Brunskill R W 1978: *Illustrated Handbook of Vernacular Architecture,* Faber and Faber, London.

Curl J S (2006, 2nd edition) *Oxford Dictionary of Architecture and Landscape Architecture.* Oxford: Oxford University Press.

Messenger M (2007) *North Devon Clay: The Story of an Industry and Its Railways.* Truro: Twelveheads Press.

Strong H W (1889) *Industries of North Devon.* Newton Abbot: David and Charles

Bronze Age

Named for and defined by its distinctive technology, the Bronze Age on the European mainland dates from around 3500 BC, but in Britain from around 1000 years later. The Early Bronze Age in the British Isles was marked by the adoption of what archaeologists call the 'Beaker culture', which had arrived from continental Europe. The term is based on the distinctively shaped drinking vessels found in burials of the early Bronze Age. Beaker-using communities were the earliest metallurgists in Britain and Ireland, their products including artefacts of both copper and gold. The addition of tin to copper to produce a harder metal alloy had already been discovered on the Continent, and it was in this late Neolithic early Bronze Age so-called Beaker period that the technology became established in Britain. Copper ore was mined in, for example, North Wales and in Ireland, which was also a source of gold, while tin was extracted in Cornwall and Devon and traded with the Continent. During the roughly two millennia of the British Bronze Age the metal was used for the production of axes, sickles, knives and daggers, swords and spears as well as items of personal adornment. This is not to say that the ancient flint technology disappeared and in fact barbed and tanged flint arrowheads as well as discoidal 'scrapers' are characteristic Bronze Age artefacts. When the North Devon Archaeological Society excavated a Middle Bronze Age settlement near Parracombe, North Devon no evidence was found of the use of metal, while it was apparent that flint was in everyday use. On the other hand bronze was not absent from northern Devon, as the finds by metal detectorists of bronze 'palstaves' (axe-heads) testify.

Relative to other prehistoric periods, the evidence of Bronze Age activity in Devon is widespread and plentiful. Having said this, most of the known evidence is found on the moors and uplands, principally Dartmoor, where barrows, the remains of settlements and field-systems have been preserved. On Dartmoor the systems of 'reaves', long, straight, parallel boundaries within and between which are hut circles, while the marks of individual fields, imply strong central organisation. Correspondingly it is thought that the shift from Neolithic communal burial in long barrows to individual burials of cremated remains beneath round barrows is a symptom of the development of social hierarchies. At the pinnacle of such societies may have been chieftain dynasties whose members' remains were placed beneath barrows in high, prominent locations. Thus we find barrow cemeteries at, for example, Five Barrows on the high rim of Exmoor, at Wrangworthy Cross and on Bursdon Moor, all of which command views over swathes of the Northern Devon countryside. (TG)

Building stone and Cob

As W G Hoskins (1972) notes, Northern and Mid–Devon do not possess outstanding building stone, although stone adequate for basic construction and relatively unsophisticated building could be found almost everywhere. What Northern Devon does lack is a stone with suitable properties for dressing to form elegant ashlar blocks and so where this has been required, the stone has almost invariably been brought from further afield. Northern Devon has a ready supply of sandstones and shales from both the Devonian rocks laid down from about 380 million years ago to the north of Barnstaple and South Molton and from the Carboniferous rocks dating from c. 350 to c. 290 million years ago lying to the south, although these latter rocks are as often shales and really only suitable for rougher work. Among the stone of Devonian origin, the most favoured for relatively formal purposes appears to have been the purple-ish Pickwell

Devonian shale, either Morte or Ilfracombe slate, a poor quality building stone.

Mixed Devonian shales and sandstones showing two different periods of build at Shirwell parish church.

Down sandstone. The Devonian rocks include the Morte Slates, which have been used to supply roofing slate (traditionally called 'hele stones'). Even as early as the seventeenth century, higher quality Delabole slate from Cornwall was used on some buildings and then slate from North Wales became available after the arrival of the railways from c 1860. Delabole slate is silvery grey in colour, while Welsh slate is blue or purple.

The one superior building stone in Northern Devon is Lundy granite which is of Eocene age (c 52 Ma). Quarries were established on Lundy in 1863 and worked until 1872 and an extensive network of tramways and inclined planes built. Loading ships from the island was always problematic and made the venture commercially precarious but some granite blocks did find their way from Lundy to the Thames embankments in London. Traces of the track-bed and the inclined planes and winding houses can be found but the actual quarry faces have largely returned to a semi-natural state. Some quarrying clearly predated the Victorian era as Lundy granite was used in several churches, including, Alwington, Clovelly, Parkham and Woolsery. Some granite was also brought from Dartmoor. Such is the nature of quarrying that more recent activity usually obliterates older workings, while the dressing and cleaning up of stone often takes place where it is to be used and not at the quarry site. As its heyday was so short, Lundy has the best surviving archaeology of quarrying along its east coast (SS138 451 and northwards).

A peculiarity of Northern Devon is the use of quartz, locally known as spar rock. This shiny white crystalline material occurs as veins and bands, often quite massive, running through the body of the shales and sandstones. Its shining white appearance seems to have caught the eye of Neolithic and Bronze Age people who used it as standing stones or as the kerb stones around burial mounds. In the Victorian era it was widely used for decorative purposes. Large irregular blocks of quartz are sometimes seen as the foundation layer in the walls of old buildings.

Quartz blocks (spar rock) at the base of a shale built wall near Combe Martin.

Many of the new turnpike roads cut in the first half of the nineteenth century used stone dug locally and overgrown quarries can be seen along many of them, such as at Chestwood (SS564 311), just outside Barnstaple. Other quarries were worked around Combe Martin in Devonian limestones and along a band of Carboniferous limestone running from Venn (SS580 305), near Barnstaple through to Irishborough (SS640 282), SE of Swimbridge. The limestone quarried here was burnt for use in lime mortar or for agricultural fertiliser.

Up until the early 20th century lime mortar was the regular bonding material in stone and brick construction, but was eventually replaced by Portland cement. In earlier periods (pre-19th century) when lime was either unavailable or too expensive, a mixture of clay and lime was used to bond stonework. This relatively poor clay-lime is surprisingly durable and can be recognised by its crumbly texture and pale buff colour.

In addition to stone, Devon has a strong tradition of building in cob, which is simply mud and has everything in common with traditional building methods and materials from all over the world. Peter Beacham states that cob is 'the traditional means of mass wall construction throughout much of rural Devon (from the) fourteenth to the nineteenth century'. Cob is a mixture of sub-soil, straw, an aggregate such as shillet (broken down shale) and to a certain extent dung with water added to make a stiff 'mud' sometimes pounded together by cattle treading. Walls are constructed by raising successive layers of the wet mix over a stone footing, perhaps between shutters, allowing one 'lift' to harden before adding the next, the shuttering being raised as the construction progresses. When the wall is complete and the cob

Gable end of a barn in cob with stone footing Pristacott, Tawstock parish.

dried out, it is faced with a thick lime render and, given a well-built stone footing and a thatch or slate roof - 'a good hat and a good pair of boots', it is a durable, weather-proof and ensures warmth in winter and coolness in summer. Once dismissed as a 'primitive' material, cob is now admired by progressive builders and individually designed, environmentally sound new-builds can occasionally be encountered. (JB)

Further Reading

Beacham P (ed.). 1995: *Devon Building: An Introduction to Local Traditions*, Tiverton: Devon Books.

Hoskins W G (1972, 2nd edition) *Devon*. Newton Abbot: David and Charles

Rothwell P and Ternstrom M (2008) *The Lundy Granite Company: An Industrial Adventure*. Appledore: Westwell.

Canals

Canals came late to North Devon and enjoyed only a brief hey-day before railways supplanted them. Although there were several abortive proposals for a canal to link the Taw and the Exe,

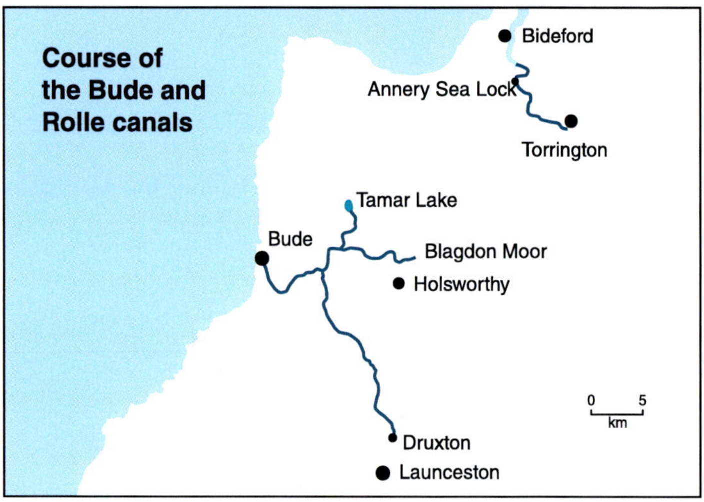

Bridge over the Rolle Canal providing access to Beam House.

only two canals were finally built and both have traces that are often quite hard to find. Both shared the same engineer, James Green, Devon's first County Surveyor, and had many similar characteristics. The earlier canal was the Bude Canal, which ran from Bude to Marhamchurch and then across the watershed to the Tamar valley, where one branch followed the river to Druxton, about 5 km north of Launceston. A second branch ran to Blagdon Moor Wharf (SS361 057) north-east of Holsworthy and had a feeder from the Lower Tamar Lake (SS295 110) which was built to supply water. This opened in 1823 and operated until 1891, when the land was sold off, although the Tamar Lake and the feeder canal were acquired by Bude UDC for water supply. The second canal was the Rolle Canal, which ran from the river Torridge at Annery Sea-Locks (SS458 233) to New Town Mills, Torrington (SS499 181). This opened in 1827 but was closed in 1871 so that the Bideford to Torrington railway could occupy some of its route.

Both canals were technically tub-boat canals and both had no other locks than the sea-locks in Bude harbour and at Annery (SS458 234) which gave access to the canals. Instead, gradients were ascended by means of inclined planes, worked by water-

Virworthy Wharf on the Tamar Lake branch of the Bude Canal.

power and drawing the wheeled tub-boats up on rails before re-floating them in the higher level. The Rolle Canal had a single inclined plane at Ridd, rising some 40 feet (c 12 metres) and with a length of 220 feet (c.67 metres). The site is not currently accessible, although an information board stands beside the Tarka Trail (SS463 224). On the Bude canal, the inclined plane at Vealand (SS283 065) is some 500 feet (c 150 metres) long and rises 58 feet (c 17.7 metres). The outline of the basin at the top of the incline and the incline itself are still visible and the tow-path is now a public right of way from Vealand Bridge at the entrance to Devon Wildlife Trust's nature reserve (SS291 067). The Bude Canal was built to a standard 19 feet (c 5.8 metres) width at the surface and 10 feet (c 3 metres) wide at the bottom with just 3 feet (1 metre) of water, with the Rolle Canal being just a fraction narrower. The tub boats themselves were 20 feet (c 6 metres) long and 5 feet 6 inches (c 1.7 metres) wide and drew just 1 foot 8 inches (c 0.5 metres) when fully laden with 5 tons of cargo. A horse could draw 4 tub-boats fully laden and 6 tub-boats empty. Both canals were constructed to allow lime and sea-sand to be moved inland for agricultural purposes and both canals also conveyed coal for domestic use and for limekilns. The Rolle Canal crossed the river Torridge at Beam (SS 474 209) by way of an aqueduct, which is now the driveway to Beam House and can be seen from the Tarka Trail. The access to Beam House was carried over the canal by means of a bridge which can be seen at SS475 206. (JB)

Further reading:
Harris H & Ellis M (1972) *The Bude Canal.* Newton Abbot: David and Charles
Hughes B D (2006) *Rolle Canal and the North Devon Limestone Trade*. Bideford: Edward Gaskell

Catch Meadows (or Float Meadows)

The observant walker in the North Devon countryside will occasionally have noticed, when looking across a valley, parallel grooves running horizontally across pasture fields. These are called field-gutters or catch-water leats and they belong to a system of 'catch meadows' or 'float meadows'. These devices were introduced into the pastoral landscape probably in the 17th century and continued in use, in some cases, into the 20th century. The system is not to be confused with water meadows which were developed beside rivers, though the benefit to the stock farmer is similar, namely to increase the yield of grassland.

The catch meadow system was designed for steeply sloping ground with natural watercourses carrying water down hill. The method adopted was to dig quite shallow parallel channels beginning at the natural watercourse and running along the contour maintaining a very gentle fall. At the point where the

View of a field-gutter crossing a hillside on the Arlington estate. The water would come from a streamlet hidden among the trees on the right.

channel or leat originated a sluice was inserted usually consisting of little more than a slab of stone that could be lifted or removed. From autumn to early spring each year the sluice could be opened when required and water could be diverted from the watercourse to flow along the leat. Sods were placed in the leat to control the flow, encouraging it to spill over a low ridge on the downhill side, gently flooding the ground below. This would keep the frost off and allow the soil te mperature to rise encouraging grass to grow on through the winter and in the spring to give an 'early bite'. Often a carriage gutter was dug to divert water through the stockyard, carrying with it nutrients from the animal waste. In at least one Northern Devon example the old domestic privy is built out over the carriage gutter which feeds the leats.

Well established by the end of the 18th century, the system was widely adopted on Exmoor and in Northern Devon in the 19th century, as estates promoted agricultural improvement. At

Emmetts Grange, one of the Knights' farms on Exmoor, the estate manager Robert Smith made extensive use of the system in his efforts to convert moorland into pasture. (TG)

For an illustration of a field-gutter in use see Riley and Wilson-North 2001, page 128.

Chapels (Non-conformist)

Chapels are a very distinctive feature of the Northern Devon landscape reflecting the strength in the nineteenth century of Protestant dissent in the area. The earliest congregations in Barnstaple and Bideford date from after the 1662 Act of Uniformity, when Puritan clergy were evicted from their livings in the parish churches. At Bideford, Lavington Church in Bridgeland Street is home to the successor congregation, although the present building dates only from 1869. Most of Northern Devon's non-conformist chapels originated in Methodism, although a few were built by the Baptists. The Wesley brothers, John and Charles and George Whitefield, effectively founders of Methodism, preached throughout Devon in the latter part of the eighteenth century. Most Methodist chapels were built as Methodism itself fragmented into different denominations in the early nineteenth century. Northern Devon's very own Methodist denomination, the Bible Christians, owed its origin to preaching at Shebbear of a dissident Methodist minister, William O'Bryan in 1815. O'Bryan's strong personality proved divisive and he in turn was ousted from his new church and leadership fell to James Thorne, who is commemorated in the James Thorne Memorial Chapel in Bear Street, Barnstaple, built in 1876 and now known as Christ Church, following the union of the Methodist and United Reform Church congregations in the town in 1988. With several waves of religious revivalism in the nineteenth century, non-conformity attracted significant numbers of

Wesleyan chapel built in 1838 at Lana, Pancrasweek.

adherents, especially among the poorer labouring and fishing classes. A mixture of hostility from Anglican land-owners and a practical awareness of the distribution of chapel going people, meant that many chapels were built at cross-roads such as at Ebberley Hill (SS570 194) or in subordinate settlements such as Lower Lovacott in Fremington parish (SS520 274) and in one case precisely on the parish boundary as with Hope (SS306 235), a former Bible Christian chapel between Clovelly Cross and Hartland. Most of the chapels were relatively small buildings, with a plain, even austere finish, and some eschewed stained glass-windows as being too redolent of popery. Economic and social change caused rural depopulation from the mid nineteenth century and as poorer people tended to be among the earlier emigrants and also chapel goers, many chapels found their congregations in steep decline. In 1907, three Methodist denominations, including the Bible Christians, merged to form the United Methodist Church. In Northern Devon a few chapels were closed as part of this rationalisation and many more were to go in the years after 1932, when the United Methodists, Wesleyans and Primitive Methodists reunited to form the modern Methodist church. Rationalisation and chapel closures were further made necessary because of falling congregations as part of a wider decline in religious observance through the twentieth century. Now as characteristic as the wayside Methodist chapel is a former chapel, converted into a dwelling house and sometimes extended. (JB)

Further Reading: **Cherry B** and **Pevsner N** 2002: The Buildings of England: Devon, Yale University Press

Christianity

In the area of Northern Devon the evidence of 'early' or 'Celtic' Christianity - brought initially by missionaries from South Wales and Ireland - comes in a variety of forms. Firstly comes local tradition. This may be regarded as the weakest evidence because it is essentially legend, but supplemented by relatively hard archaeological evidence, it deserves respect. The churches at Stoke (Hartland), Braunton and Chittlehampton are dedicated to saints Nectan, Brannoc and Urith or Hieritha respectively all of whom have legends attached to their names which appear to reach back to pre-Saxon times and which associate them firmly with the places where their churches stand. Landkey preserves the name of St Kea, a Cornish saint whose influence spread as far as Somerset.

The earliest churches recorded in Devon were minsters, probably home to a 'college' of priests living communally and serving the spiritual needs of a scattered rural community. It is very likely that at Stoke (Hartland) and it is certain that at Braunton there were 'minsters', originating perhaps as early as the 6th century. The evidence for minsters at these places is that at Stoke there was a community of 'canons' whose existence is well documented, while it is known from a 9th century charter that Braunton was known as 'Brannocmynster'. South Molton may also have housed a minster, for here too there is documentary evidence for a college of priests.

Very early churches, or at least consecrated graveyards, may

Ruins of the Augustinian priory at Frithelstock.

have existed at Landkey and Landcross, as both of these places contain in their names the Brittonic lann referring to a circular or subcircular Christian graveyard. It is suggested by Susan Pearce that the –stow in the place-names Instow, Petrockstow, Virginstow, etc represents a translation into English of lann, so that these places too may have had early churches or at least places of Christian assembly.

Once Devon became politically part of Wessex in the 7th/8th century, any remnants of the distinctively 'Celtic' church and its practices were superseded by the norms of the church of Rome whose English base was at Canterbury. In the late 7th century King Cenwalh of Wessex founded an English minster at Exeter and in the early 8th century the new diocese of Sherborne was directing events in Devon. In the time of King Ine of Wessex (late 7th to early 8th century), Glastonbury Abbey was receiving grants of land in Devon and in 729 was granted land in the Torridge valley. In the mid 9th century Brannocmynster or Braunton was granted to Glastonbury Abbey 'for the taking of fish'. In succeeding centuries, monastic influence became widespread in Devon. The probable minster at Hartland (Stoke) was succeded by the foundation in 1157 of the Augustinian abbey of Hartland, in the 12th century the priory at Pilton was founded by Malmesbury Abbey, Tavistock Abbey, founded in 981, acquired lands at Hatherleigh, Burrington and Abbotsham, the monks of Montacute held land at Monkleigh, Ford Abbey held Lynton, an Augustinian priory was established at Frithelstock, the French abbey of Cluny near Paris had an outpost in the Cluniac priory of Barnstaple. Meanwhile the See of Sherborne spawned a new bishopric based initially on Crediton, subsequently transferring to Exeter. In 1086 (Domesday Book) the Bishops of Exeter held the valuable manors of Bishops Tawton and Bishops Nympton.

The tower and spire of St Brannocks Church at Braunton, said by Pevsner to be one of the most interesting churches in North Devon.

It is very noticeable that in the vast majority of rural parishes the church stands next to or very close to the manor house or at least to the 'town' or barton farm, in the cases of Warkleigh and Satterleigh right beside the farmyard. This is strongly suggestive of the context in which they were founded. While you will find on the wall of most churches a list of incumbents beginning in the 13th century, this simply represents the period in which records become consistently informative. The great refashioning of churches in the perpendicular style of the 15th century masks their beginnings which in most cases very probably go back to the pre-Conquest period, though as stone-buildings probably to the 11th to 13th centuries. In the 10th and 11th centuries it appears that there was a wave of church building right across England as secular lords established churches to serve their families and their dependent communities. This was probably the period in which parishes were carved out of earlier larger territories. In this context it may be that the more powerful thegns sought to ensure their own and their dependents' spiritual well-being by building churches or it may be that they sought to wrest power from the hitherto controlling minsters. Whatever the motive, it appears to have become the custom to build a church conveniently close to the manorial centre (manor house or barton) as we see today at, for instance Marwood, Fremington, Clovelly, Parracombe (the old church), Clawton, Tawstock and many others. Having said this, there are places where the reverse may have happened, the Lord of the Manor building his house next to an established church or holy place, as perhaps at Landkey, and Instow, where there are suggestions of an early lann.

The most obvious archaeological evidence of the development of Christian Devon is represented by the churches themselves. The design of churches developed throughout the Middle Ages from the relative simplicity and restraint of the early Norman period with its Romanesque rounded arches and massive columns through the stylistic developments known as Early English, then Decorated, then Perpendicular. Apart from some doorways (see below) and numerous fonts, examples of the Norman style are hard to find in our area. In fact in most of our churches any evidence of the earliest periods was swept away in the great rebuilding of the 15th/16th century in the Perpendicular style (The church of St Nectan at Stoke is a fine example of this.) The work of earlier times was further obscured in the 19th century when the Anglican revival gave rise to a rash of church restorations. To anyone poking round a parish church to seek evidence of its early history, the work of the Victorian restorers can be a source of great annoyance, though to be fair they were in many instances making good the neglect of centuries; and after all, they would proclaim, the church was not a monument but a house of God for the living.

For anyone interested, there are plentiful sources of information on church architecture as well as the very valuable work by Pevsner and Cherry on the buildings of Devon. Meanwhile here are a few interesting features - selected at random and without prejudice - to look out for in the churches of our region.

Norman arch with beak-heads at Buckland Brewer.

At Braunton the church has an unusual 'broach spire' (likewise Barnstaple parish church and Swimbridge) dendrochronologically dated to 1275. In the vestry at the base of the tower is a small lancet window the lintel over which is what appears to be part of the shaft of a Saxon preaching cross or perhaps a gravestone. The carved bench ends in the unusually broad nave are full of interest. Very fine carving is also to be seen at Alwington and Landcross.

The ground plan of most churches involves a long nave with north and south aisles and the chancel at the east end. Between the nave and the chancel is an area known as the transept. Normally the church tower is at the west end, but in a few instances the tower is over the transept either centrally or laterally. Transeptal towers are to be seen at, for example, Abbotsham, Barnstaple, Fremington, Ilfracombe, Mortehoe, Shirwell. At High Bickington it is evident that a transeptal tower has been taken down and has been replaced by a west end tower, clearly indicating that the transeptal tower came first. At Ilfracombe there is evidence within the building that the transeptal tower was once detached. The tower at Braunton is also on the south side of the building, but there is no transept. Tawstock and Bishops Tawton have a central tower, perhaps following the cruciform plan of the earliest church on the site. Lateral towers are something of a Northern Devon feature and together with central towers appear to be of greater antiquity than the standard west end tower.

At Shebbear, Wolfardisworthy, Parkham and Buckland Brewer the south door retains a Norman arch (11th/12th century). At Buckland Brewer the arch is particularly fine with so-called 'beak-heads', carved heads of wolves and ravens together with human faces.

Very fine carved rood screens are to be seen at Swimbridge, Pilton, Combe Martin, Stoke (Hartland) and Marwood among others. Look for a hidden Green Man.

At Cheriton in Brendon parish there is no church despite the fact that the name means 'church ton'. There is a church site, but it is believed that the church was dismantled in the late 18th century and the material used to build or rebuild a church at Brendon. Rather similarly at Cheristow in Hartland there was once a chapel (recorded in 1198, now long since disappeared) dedicated to Saint Wen, yet another saintly figure from South Wales. This was one of six ancient chapels in Hartland parish.

Apart from churches, many a medieval manor house had its private chapel or oratory, licensed by the Bishop and served by either a resident priest or one who regularly visited to conduct mass. A well preserved medieval oratory is to be seen at Honiton Barton in South Molton parish and also at Lower Alfardisworthy in Bradworthy parish. Both are now used as agricultural buildings. Different from private oratories are chantry chapels, where a priest would sing mass for the sake of a deceased person's soul. St Anne's chapel in Barnstaple began life as a chantry.probably in the early 14th century.

For most people chapels are. places of worship associated with Methodism and other dissenting traditions which arose after the 16th century. For these, see the entry 'Chapels'.

Finally, until well into the modern period the parish church and priest were supported by 'tithes', that is a tenth part of the produce of the parish which had to be donated to the Church. 'Great tithes (corn, grain, hay and wood) were due to the rector and 'small tithes' (everything else) to the vicar. (See the separate entry: Tithe Maps). As well as tithes, the priest would have his glebe, land owned by the Church and which he was expected to cultivate. (At East Worlington it is known that the rector cultivated his glebe well into the 20th century.) Glebeland exists in all parishes, though now frequently sold off to private owners and developers, its memory preserved sometimes in the names of housing estates. Another clue to location of glebeland is the term 'centry', corrupted from Latin *sanctuarium* 'holy ground'. Thus we find in Bishops Tawton Centry Lane, in Bittadon parish is Centery Farm, while in Hatherleigh is Sanctuary Lane running along the edge of glebeland. Similarly numerous place-names containing a form of 'priest' such as Priestacott or Preston probably point to what was once church land. (TG)

Further Reading:
Cherrey B and Pevsner N 2002: *The Buildings of England: Devon*, Yale University Press
Coulter J 1993: *Ancient Chapels of North Devon*, Barnstaple.
Higham R 2008: *Making Anglo-Saxon Devon*, Exeter, The Mint Press.
Orme N 2013: *The Church in Devon 400-1560*, Exeter, Impress Books.
Pearce S 2004: *South-western Britain in the Early Middle Ages,* Leicester University Press.
Turner S *Making a Christian Landscape*, Exeter University Press

Domesday Book

The Domesday Book of 1086 is an important, if sometimes enigmatic source for examining the rural landscape of the medieval period. It was commissioned first as an assessment of the tax revenues the king might expect, but in its current form, it is also a sort of original title deed for the estates the Normans had come to control in the years after 1066.

When we speak of the Domesday Book, we usually mean the Exchequer Domesday, but for the south- western counties, principally Devon and Cornwall, but also Somerset and Dorset, there exists also a separate Liber Exoniensis or Exeter Book of which only one copy remains in existence. It represents an earlier stage of data collection and is more detailed – especially about livestock – than the 'Great' or Exchequer Domesday. For this reason it is invaluable to researchers in the South-west. Entries are in abbreviated Latin and follow a fairly uniform pattern. For each manor, the document gives an estimate of the total potential arable land, the actual amount of land under the

Two pages of the *Liber Exoniensis* or Exeter Book listing manors held by Baldwin the Sheriff. (Reproduced by permission of the Dean and Chapter of Exeter Cathedral)

plough, areas of meadow, pasture and woodland, the division of the manor into the lord's demesne and lands of the lower tenants, and the number of presumed heads of households and numbers of livestock, usually cattle, sheep, goats and pigs. Entries are organised by land-owner and then for each feudal tenant. It is usual to list manors in a set order by the hundred in which they were located. Thus it is possible to distinguish, for instance, just which of the several Torringtons is being dealt with by reference to the names of other manors before and after the entry. What the Domesday Book does not do is give any indication of the precise boundaries of manors. Some manors appear subsequently to have become ecclesiastical parishes, but other manors now lie within one or more ecclesiastical parishes and it is not possible, when a modern ecclesiastical parish contains more than one Domesday manor, to be at all precise about where the boundaries between them may have lain.

Domesday Book also does not seem to include all the land, so that the 'waste', or land uncultivated and not in formal arable, pastoral or woodland management, is a residue of considerable extent. For Northern Devon, perhaps 30% of the land was waste.

Problems arise, however, around Exmoor and it seems that pasture in the Royal Forest of Exmoor was also included within the adjoining manors and it is not possible to rule out double counting, where more than one manor had pasturing rights on the same tract of land on the Royal Forest.

Nonetheless, it is possible to make some estimates of land-use in Northern Devon in the late eleventh century. These are shown in the Table below and it is striking just how little woodland was recorded. (JB)

Land-use in Northern Devon in the Domesday Book

Land use	Area (acres)	Percentage of total
Arable	219,170	43.3
Meadow	11,048	2.2
Pasture	102,745	20.3
Woodland	20,951	4.1
Waste	152,683	30.1

Further reading:

For a text and translation of the Devon entries:

Thorn C & F (1985) *Domesday Book: Devon.* (2 volumes). Chichester: Philimore

Darby H C and Welldon Finn R (eds) 1967: *The Domesday Geography of South-West England*, Cambridge.

Welldon Finn R (1973) *Domesday Book: A Guide.* Chichester: Philimore.

Enclosures

Archaeologists and landscape historians use the term 'enclosure' in a variety of contexts. In general the meaning of the term is obvious: the enclosing of an area of ground with a boundary or barrier. The particular purposes for such an act may however be various, ranging from the protective enclosure of a homestead to the enclosure of hitherto open common land (the 18th and 19th

Voley Castle: an embanked and ditched hillslope enclosure near Parracombe, probably of Iron Age date.

century parliamentary 'inclosures') for the purpose of agricultural improvement.

The need or desire to enclose land or homesteads may have arisen with the development of farming in the Neolithic period. Enclosures may be made for the purposes of defence against enemies, defence against wild or domestic animals or they may serve to demarcate territory and to reinforce personal or group identity.

In Devon prehistoric enclosures fall roughly into two types: hilltop and hillslope enclosures. Hilltop enclosures comprise a broad spectrum from Hembury hillfort in East Devon, a multivallate (ie. with two or more banks) hillfort in the Wessex Iron Age tradition, to simple earth-banked enclosures on hilltops such as Beacon Castle near Parracombe (SS665 460). Somewhere in between are sturdily built promontory forts such as Windhill at Countisbury and Hillsborough at Ilfracombe and, for example, the much slighter Berry Castle near Huntshaw

(SS495 223). Such disparate structures tend to be lumped together as 'hillforts', a debatable identification which is treated in a separate entry.

The rest of this entry concentrates on 'hillslope enclosures'. The term was coined by Lady Aileen Fox to cover all ovoid or sub-rectangular enclosures – of highly variable size – situated on hillsides and which are clearly not hillforts. Good, readily visible examples are Voley Castle near Heale, Parracombe(SS656 463), Smythapark near Arlington (SS637 384) or Roborough, south-east of Barbrook in Lynton parish (SS731 460). Easily accessible and very well preserved is one to the east of Chawleigh at SS742 126. Numerous examples (often labelled simply 'Settlement') can be found by studying the Explorer Series OS maps at 1:25 000 and many more have been recorded under favourable conditions by aerial photography.

These small enclosures, frequently defined by a surrounding earth bank and a ditch, have been little explored, but very probably represent enclosed settlements which are usually assumed to be of late prehistoric (Iron Age) date. However, the only two that have been excavated confound this assumption. At Rudge, Morchard Bishop a hillslope enclosure excavated by Malcolm Todd in the 1980s turned out to be Romano-British, while another excavated by North Devon Archaeological Society in 2002-5 at Holworthy Farm near Parracombe was radio-carbon dated to the Middle Bronze Age (around 1200 BC). These two examples strongly suggest that the tradition of settlement enclosure endured for a good 2000 years. The Holworthy enclosure also failed to conform to the theoretical 'norm' because its enclosing bank was of piled rubble stone and there was no ditch. (Similarly stone embanked enclosures, apparently of the Bronze Age, are seen on Dartmoor.) Within the enclosure was a circle of post-holes probably representing a roundhouse, and it is assumed that other such enclosures will also contain one or more roundhouses as well as workshops and animal pens.

Apart from these two enclosures, the best that can be said for their period of origin is that they are 'prehistoric' up to early medieval, belonging to the period c.1500 BC up to and beyond the Roman period (AD 43- AD 410). During this long period, an evolution of form and quite possibly function and social status will have occurred, so that we see a varied geometry from completely round to variations on the quadrilateral. This variety may have significance and may offer clues to chronology, but the necessary exploratory work remains to be done. The evidence of prehistoric enclosures is very often best or only seen from the air. Good examples from across Devon may be found in Frances Griffith's 1988 work 'Devon's Past; An Aerial View' (pages 34-47). (TG)

Further Reading:

Green T 2009: Excavation of a Hillslope Enclosure at Holworthy Farm, Parracombe displaying Bronze Age and Iron Age Activity, in *Proceedings of the Devon Archaeological Society*, No. 67.

Grinsell L V 1970: *The Archaeology of Exmoor: Bideford Bay to Bridgwater*, David and Charles.

Griffith F 1988: *Devon's Past: An Aerial View*, Exeter, Devon Books.

Factories

Although it seems obvious that manufacturing should take place in a factory or at least a workshop, for most of Northern Devon's history its manufacturing was on a smaller scale and often occurred in domestic settings. Thus the extensive woollen industry, for which the area was famous for much of the period 1200 – 1800, has left very little evidence, other than in place names such as tucking mill (see mills) and the family name Tucker. Factories employing several hundred people on a single site came to Northern Devon in the nineteenth century, with perhaps the best known being the Derby Lace Factory in

Derby lace factory, Barnstaple 1971.

Vicarage Street, Barnstaple (SS563 336) built in 1825. The building was badly damaged by a fire in 1972 and just three of the original twelve bays survive to the full height of four stories. Glove making was another industry to be organised on a factory scale, although it also employed nearly as many domestic outworkers, particularly in villages around Great Torrington, such as Langtree, Peters Marland, Petrockstow and Sheepwash, as it did in factories. Vaughan's Glove Factory in White's Lane Torrington (SS494 192) was built in 1884 and looks rather like an enlarged non-conformist chapel. It cut out the gloves from pieces of leather and the gloves themselves were sent to outworkers to be sewn up. One factor behind the location of the glove industry in the area was the supply of leather, itself an obvious product of a livestock economy. Devon was important nationally in the nineteenth century for leather making and Northern Devon had 19 tanneries, with noted concentrations in Barnstaple, South Molton and Torrington. Tanneries were particularly susceptible to fires, which destroyed that in Holsworthy in 1841 and another in Bear Street Barnstaple in 1849. The last tanneries to survive were those at Swimbridge and South Molton, which closed in 1965. Another Northern

Devon industry that has died out is collar making. A factory occupying a former flour mill was opened by Vincent and Duncan in Westcombe, Bideford (SS 450 269) in 1873 and extended soon afterwards. At its peak, the factory employed almost 400 people but changing fashions led to its closure in the 1920s. The malting of barley for beer was widespread in Devon with at least 14 maltings in Northern Devon, including those in Barnstaple, Bideford, Ilfracombe, South Molton and Torrington and in villages such as Chittlehampton and Hartland. None has survived with the characteristic ventilator intact. Perhaps the last 'traditional factory' is the Raleigh Cabinet Works of Shapland and Petter by the south bank of the river Taw in Barnstaple (SS

Vaughan's glove factory, Great Torrington.

556 329). The name indicates that the original factory lay at Raleigh on the northern edge of the town and the current factory in white Marland brick was constructed after the original factory was destroyed by fire in 1888. Only one of the two blocks now survives and the future of this is tied up with plans for the redevelopment of the site, now that all manufacturing has ceased. (JB)

Further reading:
Bodman M (2009) Tanning in Devon in the nineteenth century. *Transactions of the Devonshire Association.* 141. 219-236.
Strong H W (1889)(reprinted 1971 with introduction by B D Hughes) *Industries of North Devon.* Newton Abbot: David and Charles.

Farms, Farmhouses and Farm Buildings:

In a very rural area such as Northern Devon, farms are the most frequently encountered settlement form, so that an understanding of their dynamic can take the interested observer a long way towards understanding the landscape. This entry will therefore look briefly at the evolution of the farm, the development of its characteristic main residence and the form and functions of its buildings.

The vast majority of farms in northern Devon have names which are recorded in medieval documents from 1086 (Domesday) onwards. In the earlier medieval period they would have existed as tenements within the manorial system, their occupants dependent on and owing service to the Lord of the Manor. It must be understood that the manor was an area of land, not just the manor house, but at its heart was the demesne farm (barton farm or home farm) comprising land which the lord retained for his own use, but which was worked by the peasantry. After the Black Death in the 14th century the grip of manorial lords was loosened, allowing the medieval peasant to develop

A typical cross-passage house at Croyde, service end to the right of the door, inner room to the left. The lateral chimney stack is visible to passers-by.

into the yeoman farmer (freeholder or leaseholder) free of feudal duties and with a security of tenure that made it worthwhile building a home that could house the family for several generations. Thus we find that many Devon farmhouses date from the late medieval to early post-medieval period (late 15th to early 17th century). Typically at this period the house would be built to a common design of three rooms and a cross-passage. In its earliest manifestation the house would have a passage running from front door to back door with a service room to one side and on the other side an open hall with beyond it an inner room. Above the inner room would be sleeping quarters reached by a ladder and above the service room would be storage. In the early days there would be an open fire in the centre of the hall, the smoke escaping through the thatch or through a louvred arrangement in the roof. This would result in the roof timbers and the thatch becoming smoke blackened, and in those quite rare instances where the roof has not been rebuilt, the presence today of smoke-blackened roof timbers is a good indication that the building dates from the late 15th or 16th century.

The discomfort of living in a smoky atmosphere was eventually overcome by introducing into the farmhouse an arrangement which had been known in the finer houses and castles for several centuries, namely an enclosed fireplace with a chimney. This would be located either centrally, backing onto the cross-passage or laterally on the front of the hall with an external chimney stack so that the luxurious innovation was visible to all and a proof of status.

With this novelty in place it became possible to 'ceil' over the hall, and by the introduction of stairs – often in a stair turret on the back of the building – and the suitable placing of partitions, chambers (bedrooms) were created. Thus the dynamic of domestic life was altered. Further changes followed down the centuries, but in very many Devon farmhouses the early pattern can still be made out. Typically the building has a linear arrangement of rooms producing a long house. This is NOT however a 'longhouse' – despite the claims of many an estate agent: that is something different and very rarely encountered apart from Dartmoor.

Just to be clear, the longhouse has its origins in the early medieval period and reflects a pattern seen across Europe. In this, humans and animals are accommodated under one roof. The longhouse as encountered in the upland parts of Devon – Dartmoor and to some extent Exmoor – is built into a slope having at the upper end domestic accommodation consisting at its simplest of a hall and an inner room which are separated by a cross-passage from the lower end comprising a shippon for the housing of animals. Very few indeed are definitely known in Northern Devon, though a few more are suspected beneath the accretions of later centuries.

The three-room and cross-passage house is not confined to Devon and is not exclusive to the countryside, but it is characteristic of the traditional Devonshire farm building stock.

The tradition lasted until the later 17th century when it began to make way for more 'national' fashionable styles. The 18th century – and also the 19th century - farmhouse, catering to a variety of functions and bearing an increased air of gentility, is usually built on a symmetrical floor-plan with a central entrance leading to a hallway with reception rooms on either side and a kitchen, dairy and store-rooms at the rear. Stairs lead from the hallway to the first floor where bedrooms are evenly located on either side of a landing. Externally the positioning of windows creates a look of balance and symmetry, the whole quite square. This is in fact – externally at least - a town house built in the countryside.

Depending on circumstances, the farmhouse of the 18th or 19th century might be a completely new build or might adapt and add a fashionable exterior to an earlier, traditional design. Where this is the case, the earlier features can often be detected by judicious 'poking around'. On the other hand, where the 18th or 19th century owner or tenant built anew, the shell of the older house might be relegated to use as a barn whose origins can often be determined by the quality of the roof timbers or what are quite obviously domestic windows and doorways.

Farm Buildings

The farm buildings of Devon reflect the requirements of a mixed rural economy. One could list a dozen traditional specialised buildings commonly found around Devonshire farmyards, but here we shall restrict ourselves to a few characteristic types.

Almost exclusive to Devonshire is the linhay (pronounced 'linnie'). This is an open-fronted building with evenly spaced, quite often cylindrical stone pillars supporting a 'tallet'or open-sided loft where hay is stored. From the tallet hay can be dropped into the space below where cattle can feed. The animals might also feed from a manger located along the back wall. The linhay is principally a feeding arrangement for cattle confined to the

A disused linhay near Mortehoe with characteristic cylindrical pillars.

stockyard over winter. For shelter from the weather animals may be housed in a long barn or shippon. It is relevant to mention in this context the small enclosure close to the farmyard known as the 'mowhay'. Here the hay for winter feed was stored in hayricks or stacks.

Although today Devon is principally cattle and sheep country, cereals were in the past at least equally important and every farm has buildings dedicated to processing and storing grain. Once harvested and brought in from the fields, grain crops would be housed in a corn barn. This is normally, apart from the farmhouse, the most prominent building on a farm, recognisable by its centrally placed large double doors with an opposing pair of double doors on the other side of the building. Flanking the double doors are prominent stone buttresses. These are the 'threshing cheeks', the function of which is to channel a draught of air across the threshing floor, a boarded area within the building between the two pairs of doors. In the days before machinery sheaves of corn were thrown down on this floor and threshed with flails and the draught would blow away the loosened husks, thus winnowing the grain.

In the early 19th century the arduous task of hand threshing began to be taken over by a threshing machine. The power for this was provided by horses. In an 'engine house' or 'round house' attached to the back of the barn a horse would plod around in a circle turning a central spindle which was connected by crown wheel and pinion to a shaft running through the wall of the barn to the threshing machine. Having gone out of use finally in the 1920s, they have mostly been demolished, but where it is retained, the usually semi-circular horse engine house or gin attached to the back of a threshing barn is a sign of early mechanisation on the 19th century farm. In a few rare instances – eg. at Buckland Barton north of Braunton – not only the engine house but the machinery remains. The former existence of an engine house can sometimes be detected by the presence of a large hole in the back wall of the barn and/or remnants of the circular cobbled floor.

Another typically Devonshire feature is the cider house sometimes called the pound house. Here apples from the once

Threshing barn near Challacombe showing the threshing cheeks and with semi-circular (former) horse engine house attached.

ubiquitous orchards were stored and processed to produce cider. The first part of the process was to crush the apples to a pulp. This was accomplished in a circular stone - usually granite – trough around which a horse propelled a heavy stone crushing wheel. The pulp was made up into 'cheeses' in hessian sacks which were then placed in a massive wooden press to extract the juice. Fermented in barrels, the resulting cider provided drink for the farm workers throughout the year. Such was the production of cider in Devon that many thousands of gallons were exported from the county. The cider house or pound house is not necessarily a distinctive building, but may be identified by surviving machinery – for example at Fairlynch, Braunton – or merely the knowledge that such and such a building is the 'pound house'.

Other farm buildings include the bank barn, cart shed, shelter shed, stables, pigsties, ash house and root store. Details of the use and history of these can be found in Peter Beacham's book 'Devon Building'.

The period from about 1780 onwards saw a wave of agricultural improvement. This was expressed not only through the increasing use of machinery –and a consequent reduction of the labour force -, but also, in the 19th century, through the development of'model farms'. The purpose was to overcome the handicaps imposed by buildings that had evolved over the centuries and to build anew, every building being designed to meet a specific purpose. There are not many examples in our area, but at Wistlandpound (SS645 424), now an activity centre for the disabled, the features of the model farm built by the Fortescues are clearly visible. (TG)

Further Reading:

Beacham P 1995: *Devon Building: An Introduction to Local Traditions*, Tiverton.

Hegarty C & Wilson-North R 2014: *The Archaeology of Hill Farming on Exmoor*, English Heritage.

Field Systems

When landscape archaeologists talk about 'field-systems' they are usually referring to signs of either prehistoric or medieval management of land into enclosed areas. We should probably assume that from the beginning of farming in the Neolithic period, areas of land in which to grow crops or to graze stock were somehow defined. In the beginning the practice might have been to slash and burn creating temporary forest clearings, but as areas of productive land became recognised and permanent settlement was encouraged, the forest would have been stripped away. What we would recognise as fields might then have been created by dividing up land with ditches, banks, stones or hedges. It has to be said however, that the evidence of Neolithic field-systems in England is very sparse and there is at present none recognised in Devon.

In the period of time that we call the Bronze Age however, we begin to see evidence of small fields associated with settlements. The evidence for these is usually in the form of low boundary banks just surviving in the landscape and discernible in favourable lighting conditions. These may be associated with the remnants of hut circles. In Northern Devon such evidence is found in the Valley of Rocks at Lynton (SS70-49-), on Martinhoe Common (SS67-47-) and on Holdstone Down (SS62-48-). Recent work by the National Mapping Programme has found evidence of small irregular prehistoric fields on Berry Down (Berrynarbor) possibly associated with the hillslope enclosure at North Hill Cleave (SS548 438). An interesting feature of these prehistoric systems is that they can show signs of 'centralised' organisation. On Dartmoor it was realised some years ago that prehistoric fields were arranged in a regular fashion between long, parallel boundaries known as 'reaves'. The field boundaries observed in the Valley of Rocks and other prominent examples across Exmoor have a certain regularity and may suggest a similar system in this region.

How long these fields were in use we do not know. It may well be that the tradition that they represent persisted through the later prehistoric and the Romano-British period. There is a certain amount of evidence from South Devon, but currently none in the north. The preservation of these traces of prehistoric cultivation is largely down to the abandonment of marginal areas because of climatic deterioration and their subsequent avoidance by medieval and later farmers.

When we come to the medieval period, things are very different. We now have plentiful evidence from the historic (ie. still existing) landscape. In central England this is the period of the 'open field system', in which the land around a core settlement was divided into three or four large 'fields' within which the soil was cultivated in long, parallel strips, bundles of strips making up a 'furlong'. The fields were cultivated on a three-crop rotation. Each villager was allocated a set number of strips in each field (traditionally about thirty) which they would cultivate. Allocated by lot each year, the individual holdings were widely scattered, so that no single family would end up with all the good or bad land. It used to be thought that this system was not found in Devon, but in the 1960s H.P.R. Finberg demonstrated from documentary and cartographic evidence that it had indeed been a feature of medieval Devon. For his prime example Finberg drew on the documentary record of Braunton. Finberg found evidence that the land to the south, east and west of the village had been cultivated in the manner of a three-field system, and even today Braunton Great Field, lying to the south-west of the village retains the character of an open field comprising intermixed holdings divided by low earth baulks called landsherds. Today many of the arable strips have been amalgamated, but the Great Field remains unenclosed. In fact, as Finberg indicated, what we call today the Great Field is only one third of a much more extensive system; the Second Edition OS map of 1903 provides ample evidence of long, narrow parallel strips of land to west and east of the village, many of these now

Aerial view of Braunton Great Field, one of only two surviving examples of the open-field system in England. (North Devon Athenaeum, Haggerty Collection)

turned into the plots on which post-war housing has been developed.

While Braunton Great Field retains the character of a medieval open field system, it can be demonstrated that it was not alone in Devon. A similarly extensive system existed around Brixham in South Devon (Shorter 1950). If nowhere else demonstrates such a complete 'classic' open field system, the evidence of medieval cultivation in arable strips and intermixed holdings can nevertheless be found throughout the county. Only documentary research will reveal the character of tenurial relationships, but the visual clues are easy enough to pick out. When the medieval Devonshire ploughman ploughed his strip (selion or land) of about an acre with an ox-drawn plough usually on a slope, he might be forced by the topography to start or finish with a slight veer to left or right. Over time this created strips with a characteristic bend, looking in plan view like either a reversed capital J or an elongated reversed C or a reversed S. When, in the later medieval period, bundles of strips were amalgamated and enclosed in new 'closes', the boundaries would very often retain the curvature of the strips, so that when we see on a modern map groups of fields with parallel, often curving

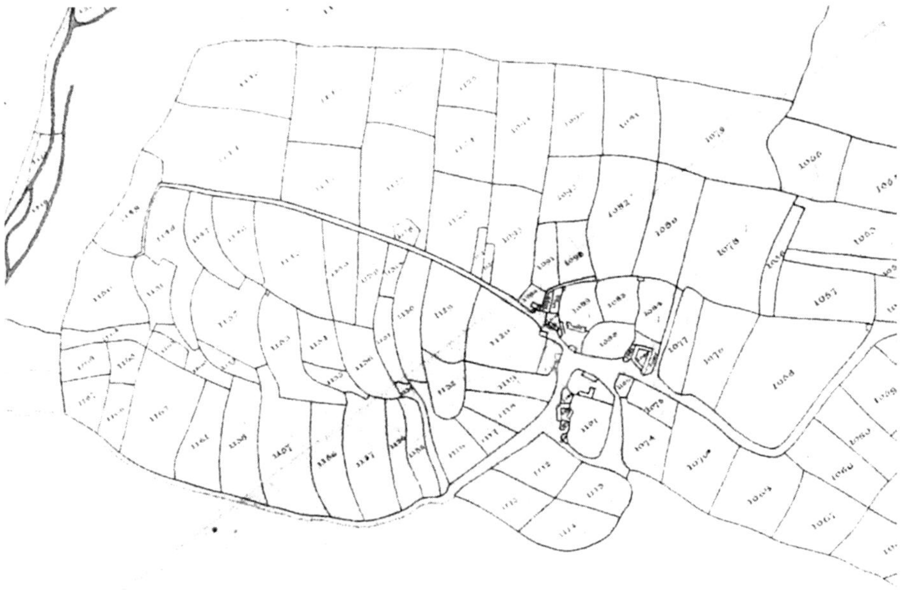

South Radworthy and its fields as recorded on the tithe map of c.1840 (DRO).

boundaries, we can be fairly sure we are looking at the ghost of a medieval field system. Such distinctive field patterns can be found associated with very many Devon hamlets, villages and towns. To take a few Northern Devon examples, recognisable groups of fields are to be found on the 1:25000 Explorer maps to the west of South Molton, around West Down, around Croyde, to the west of Frithelstock Stone, at Hiscott in Tawstock parish and extensively around Newton Tracey. In all these cases it is obvious that the strips form compact clusters. The space between would have been unenclosed land available to be ploughed intermittently, but principally to provide pasture for sheep and cattle.

Distinctively south-western and well represented in Northern Devon is evidence of an infield-outfield system also known as convertible husbandry. Simply put, the system involves the intensive year on year cultivation of an 'infield' and the occasional ploughing up and sowing of an 'outfield'. After a couple of years of cultivation the outfield is returned to grass pasture, while the infield requires the addition of manure to maintain fertility. Palaeoenvironmental evidence suggests that this system arrived in Devon at about the time of the West Saxon take-over in the early eighth century. Control of the infield might be ensured by its enclosure within a boundary, the signs of which are in some cases still visible. At South Radworthy in North Molton parish, the boundary of an ovoid enclosure is still present, but the intensity of its earlier cultivation is best evidenced by the tithe map record of about 1840. At this date the enclosure was 'stuffed' with small closes showing the characteristic curvature of enclosed medieval strips. Much the same thing can be seen at Parkham Ash (SS35-36-). Both here and at South Radworthy 19th century records indicate that the strips were held by a number of different individuals, their holdings intermixed as in the open field system. That such enclosed systems were superseded, is evident from the fact that other fields, in a number of cases also laid out originally as long strips, can be seen to spring off the enclosure boundary, indicating that the outfield eventually succumbed to permanent cultivation. Winsham (Braunton) (SS50-38-) is a good example.

In the late medieval and post-medieval period the strips of the open field were progressively enclosed, while at the same time areas of hitherto open, common land were divided up and hedged in as larger fields became the norm. The process of enclosure went on into the 18th and 19th centuries, when increasingly the private enclosure agreements of earlier centuries were superseded by enclosure through acts of parliament. A principle result of this movement was that the remaining open commons, moors and downs also became converted into fields. The marks of parliamentary enclosure are easy to pick out: wherever we find fields that are large and neatly square with geometrically straight boundaries we see its result. A very clear example of this is to be seen around Tosberry (SS262 215) and at Hendon Moor to the south of Bursdon Moor, all in Hartland

Parish. The names of late enclosed fields may be boringly prosaic, simply stating the acreage, or they may give away their earlier history when the name comprises a reference to 'moor' or 'down'. (TG)

Further Reading:
Finberg H P R 1969: The Open Field in Devon, in *West Country Historical Studies*, David and Charles, Newton Abbot
Hoskins W G 1992 edition: *The Making of the English Landscape* (with commentary by Christopher Taylor), Hodder and Stoughton, London.
Riley H and Wilson-North R 2001: *The Field Archaeology of Exmoor*, English Heritage.
Taylor C 2000 edition: *Fields in the English Landscape*, Alan Sutton, Stroud.
Shorter A H 1950: Field Patterns in Brixham, Devon, in *Transactions of the Devonshire Association* 82, 271-280.

Flint and Chert

Throughout the early history of humanity and until the arrival of metal technology, implements for cutting, chopping, piercing and shaping were fashioned from stone, bone or wood. Among suitable types of stone, flint and the very similar chert (and in other parts of the world, the glasslike obsidian, for example) were of primary importance. Both flint and chert are forms of sedimentary rock composed almost entirely of silica and laid down within geological deposits of the Cretaceous period (145 – 66 million years ago). Their usefulness is due to their dense, glasslike structure and the way they fracture when struck, lending themselves to the production of very sharp edges and points. Because of their resistance to weathering, discarded flint and chert products are durable in the soil and, to the practised eye, are easily recognised in ploughsoil or eroding cliffside or roadside deposits or on coast and moorland tracks.

Flint pebbles from Baggy Point.

The so-called 'Stone Age' comprises all of human history from the earliest manufacture of rudimentary stone tools in the Lower Palaeolithic (Old Stone Age), through the Middle and Upper Palaeolithic to the Mesolithic (Middle Stone Age), to the Neolithic (New Stone Age). However, stone technology continues throughout the Bronze Age. There are a small number of Palaeolithic artefacts known from Northern Devon, notably a large hand-axe fround near Chittlehampton. Flints from the Mesolithic and subsequent eras, on the other hand, are frequently found.

For reasons of its geological history, the Northern Devon area does not have an abundant supply of flint as raw material. Known

Neolithic and Bronze Age flint artefacts from Holworthy Farm, Parracombe. (Drawings by Brian Williams)

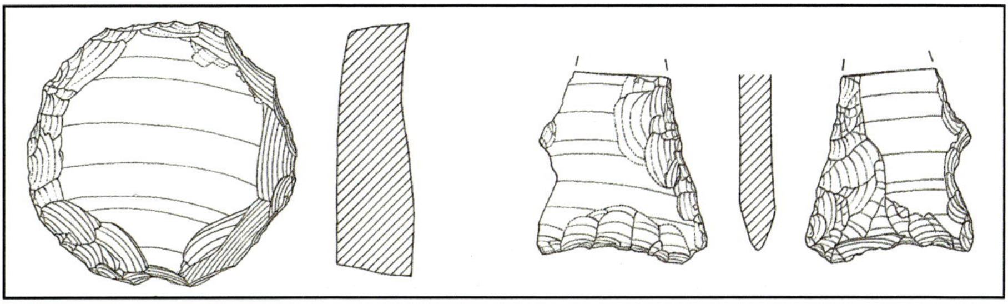

sources are a deposit of 'clay with flints' at Orleigh Court (Buckland Brewer) and beach pebbles which probably originate from Cretaceous deposits beneath the Irish Sea and are washed by tidal drift onto the beaches of Northern Devon. Another potential source has recently come to light near Petrockstow, but has yet to be fully investigated. Elsewhere in the county, the south coastal area between Beer and Salcombe Regis, the Haldon Hills and the Blackdown Hills have considerable flint or chert deposits.

However limited the sources, it is becoming more and more evident that flint and chert were in use throughout the south-west peninsula (Devon and Cornwall) in prehistory right up to the Iron Age. Whereas in the earlier, Mesolithic period much use appears to have been made of beach pebbles (the skillful use of which difficult material has to be admired), later periods probably made more use of good 'raw' flint. There is good evidence that flints and chert from South and East Devon were being transported to Northern Devon, so that distance was no obstacle when it came to such an important material.

Neolithic flint 'knife' found at Northam Burrows. Centimetre scale. (Derry Bryant)

Worked flint has been noted and collected at numerous sites in Northern Devon. In most cases these are 'debitage', that is the waste produced during the 'knapping' of a flint implement. However, it is not unusual to come across a completed article, most frequently a so-called 'scraper', perhaps a blade and occasionally an arrow-head. Some of the better known or researched sites , enumerated from west to east; and inland as far as Witheridge are:

The Stitworthy/Seckington area on the Clovelly/Hartland boundary, the cliff top area from Embury along to Elmscott and the clifftop fields at Blegberry as well as an area of East Titchberry; the intertidal foreshore at Westward Ho!; Baggy Point, where a flint knapping site was investigated by M.Townshend Hall in the mid-19th century; Kentisbury Down, where, during the first half of the 20th century, the Rev. Ayre, vicar of Kentisbury, assembled a considerable collection of flints which his sons have donated to the Museum of Barnstaple and North Devon - a very fine Neolithic polished flint discoidal knife from the collection is on display there. Farther inland recent field-walking near Merton has uncovered an extensive scatter of worked flint, while systematic field-walking near Witheridge by members of North Devon Archaeological Society has produced a large collection of worked flint implements and debitage representing a variety of sources. and occupation of the ridge above the Little Dart river over a considerable period of time.

It should be apparent from the wide distribution of these find sites – which have come to light more or less randomly – that evidence of prehistoric activity and occupation may be expected almost anywhere in our area. From Mesolithic hunter-gatherers to Neolithic and Bronze Age farmers, people have occupied the Northern Devon landscape for many thousands of years. Our knowledge of the location and distribution of the evidence is increasing all the time, and it is certain that there are many more sites which remain undiscovered or unreported. (TG and DB)

Further Reading:

Butler C 2005: *Prehistoric Flintwork*, Stroud, Tempus.

Newberry J 2002: Inland Flint in *Prehistoric Devon, in Proceedings of the Devon Archaeological Society*, Vol.60.

Gardens

Gardens and landscaped parks are a distinctive feature of the Northern Devon landscape, although they do not occupy a very large area. Parks originated in the medieval period as enclosed areas for hunting deer, and that at Clovelly Court, to the north and east of the house (SS31 25), is one such survival. As Northern Devon was a great distance from London and, by national standards, its local landed magnates were relatively impoverished, it does not have many outstanding gardens. Before the early part

The Satyr's temple, Castle Hill, Filleigh.

of the eighteenth century, gardens were formal and geometrical, involving parterres, gravel paths and statuary. The mid-eighteenth century saw major changes in garden design and all of the earlier formal gardens were replaced by what has come to be known as the English landscape garden. At Castle Hill, Filleigh (SS67 28) a major remodelling of the house and gardens was undertaken by Hugh Fortescue in the 1730s. Fortescue had travelled extensively in France and the garden clearly shows French influences in the formal avenue from the house to the triumphal arch on the hill to south. He was advised in his work by Lord Burlington and possibly by the landscape gardener, William Kent. Contemporary English influences can be seen in the Sybil's Cave grotto and the Sunrise and Sunset Temples. On his death, Hugh was succeeded by his nephew Matthew and the garden was made less formal, with the lake in front of the house re-fashioned into its present serpentine form. In the 19th century the park was extensively planted with trees and woodland.

A similar process took place in several other gardens, notably at Hartland Abbey (SS 24 25) and especially at Arlington Court

(SS61 40), where in the 1820s the old house by the church was replaced with a new house overlooking a fashionably 'picturesque' landscape where formerly had been farmland and the now swept away village of Arlington. Nineteenth century tastes saw a fondness for shrubberies, particularly of rhododendrons, and a return to rather more formal gardens, often of an Italianate style. Shrubberies survive around many of the more modest houses in Northern Devon, whilst a good example of an early twentieth century Italianate garden is at Tapeley Court (SS478 290). Saunton Court (SS457 377) was restored in 1932 by Sir Edward Lutyens and the garden was redesigned following the principles adopted by Gertrude Jeykell, his collaborator in many earlier projects. Many of the Northern Devon gentry's smaller houses have walled kitchen gardens, usually from the nineteenth century, but few now survive in

The formal Victorian garden at Arlington Court.

anything like their former condition, although at Arlington Court The National Trust has restored the walled garden to full production of fruit and vegetables. (JB)

Further reading:

Gray T 2013: *The Art of the Devon Garden*, Exeter, Mint Press

Pugsley S (ed) (1994) *Devon Gardens: An Historical Survey.* Stroud: Alan Sutton

Hillforts:

In her small, but useful publication 'Prehistoric Hillforts in Devon', Aileen Fox wrote: *A hillfort is a defended settlement enclosed by one or more ramparts built of earth dug from ditches, or built of stones; often the fortifications are conspicuous in profile in the landscape surrounding a hilltop...* This general description best fits the hillforts of Wessex, the prime example being Maiden Castle outside Dorchester. In fact very few of the Devon examples that Aileen Fox included are truly comparable with the hillforts of Wessex, the best candidate being Hembury hillfort in East Devon. On those Wessex hillforts where excavation has taken place, the evidence indicates that the classic hillforts were created in the first millennium BC – late Bronze Age into Iron Age – though many may have Neolithic precursors.

In Northern Devon the nearest thing to a classic hillfort is Clovelly Dykes (centred at SS312 234) with its concentric enclosures, its truly massive enclosing ditches and elaborate entrance, but it differs from the classic model in that it is built on a plateau and does not dominate the landscape. Lying right beside the A39 road above the village of Clovelly but hidden behind hedges, it is unknown to the majority of people who drive by. Nevertheless seen from the air it is, as Aileen Fox remarked, the most impressive prehistoric earthwork in Devon. Shoulsbury Castle (centred at SS705 391) near Brayford is morphologically close to the classic model, having double

Clovelly Dykes, aerial view from the west. (North Devon Athenaeum, Haggerty Collection)

ramparts and standing prominently on the edge of Exmoor, but it appears to be unfinished and is not readily defensible. Aileen Fox suggested that it might in fact be a stock enclosure.

Cliff castles and promontory forts are sub-classes of hillfort. We have cliff castles at Hillsborough, Ilfracombe (SS533 477), Embury, south of Hartland (SS215 195) - now almost fallen into the sea - and Windbury, Brownsham, west of Clovelly (SS286 265). These prominent features have ramparts on the landward side, but otherwise have only the cliffs and the sea at their backs. Because the Embury cliff castle is in serious danger of disappearing completely, there have been two excavations on the site, the most recent of which revealed, through the depth of the excavated ditch, the effort that its builders put into the enclosing of this windswept site.

Between Lynmouth and Countisbury is Windhill (SS740 494 mid-point of rampart), a promontory fort. Here a massive rampart has been constructed right across a ridge between the

View of the rampart of Windhill from the landward side. On the seaward side the bank and ditch descend all the way to the top of the cliff.

moor and the sea, the rampart continuing down to the cliffs on the north, seaward side. At the highest part of the rampart is a well preserved eastward facing entrance, clearly controlling movement along the coastal route. It is notable and probably significant that these features are placed to overlook and dominate parts of the rugged Northern Devon coast where a beach landing would have been possible or where a sheltered harbour was available..

Other Northern Devon sites listed by Aileen Fox as 'hillforts' (eg. Voley Castle, Parracombe, Roborough Castle, Shirwell, Mockham Down, Brayford) are hard to distinguish from hillslope enclosures and are probably enclosed farm settlements. A quite ambiguous example in our area is Berry Castle in Huntshaw Wood (SS495 221). Located on a ridge, it is larger in area than most hillslope enclosures, but has single and quite slight enclosing banks and what might be a rudimentary hornwork entrance. Such ambiguity raises the question of the function and purpose of hillforts. The term 'hillFORT' is the product of a 19th century militaristic mind-set. Certainly the classic examples are highly defensible with their formidable banks and ditches and often elaborate entrances, but where they have been excavated (notably Danebury, near Andover, Hampshire) it is clear that they are settlements with houses, workshops and even – at Danebury – a 'main street'. It should be obvious, considering the time and manpower that it must have taken to build them, that they could not have been put up in the face of an enemy. One could consider the elaborate form and visibility of the more prominent examples to be the Iron Age equivalent of the 18th century Palladian mansion displaying wealth and status. (TG)

Further Reading:
Fox A 1996: *Prehistoric Hillforts in Devon*, Exeter, Devon Books.
Griffith F 1988: *Devon's Past: An Aerial View*, Exeter, Devon Books.

Holy wells

Northern Devon has some 55 wells that have left some trace, either as archaeology or as place names or in documents. Wells and springs almost certainly had great significance in pre-Christian belief systems, but it was also relatively straight-forward to assimilate them within conventional Christianity as sources of life-giving water in baptism and as symbolic of the rock which Moses stuck in the desert to give water to the Israelites. Something of the pre-Christian probably came back when wells and springs were associated with healing and often dressed in foliage on patronal feast days. Surviving wells can be found at Stoke, Hartland (SS236 247) and Welcombe (SS228 184), both dedicated to St Nectan and at Bradworthy (SS327 139) dedicated to St Peter. Numerous 'Ladywells' ostensibly dedicated to the Virgin Mary, may in fact reflect an association of springs in pre-Christian times with a native goddess such as Coventina. The spring in Anchor Wood, Barnstaple (SS545 327), the so-

St Nectan's well, Welcombe.

called Dripping Well, was supposed to effect cures for eyes, as were many of the wells and springs in Northern Devon such as the Eye Well beside the coast path near Morte Point.(Straying for a moment well beyond our area, a well in Totnes is known as Leechwell,'leech' being an old word for 'doctor'). On Great Torrington Commons, there is a Coverney Well which was dressed with rags until the early nineteenth century, when many of the older traditions were regarded as superstitious, or worse, as residues of Catholicism, now the target of non-Conformist zeal. (JB)

Further Reading:

Orme N 2013: Medieval holy wells in Devon, in *Transactions of the Devonshire Association*, Vol.145. 155-180. (This work includes a list of holy wells in Devon recorded before 1550)

Inscribed Stones

Inscribed stones are a class of monument found principally in western Britain, Ireland and Brittany. Known in Cornish as *men scryfa*, these are personal memorials of prominent individuals dating from the 5th to 8th centuries. They are generally thought to represent a Christian expression of reverence for the dead among the elite. In the South West they are mainly found in Cornwall, but Devon has a respectable number and there is one known on Exmoor. The names on the stones are either purely Brittonic, though in a latinised form, or they are derived directly from Latin, the latter thus representing the final echoes of Romano-British culture. Very frequently the inscription is simply a name in the Latin genitive case, thus *memorial of...* or it may add *son of*. Additionally there may be a phrase *hic iacit* 'here lies...'. Most famously a stone from Castle Dore in Cornwall declares DRUSTANUS HIC IACIT CUNOMORI FILIUS, ie 'Drustanus lies here, son of Cunomorus'. This Drustanus is thought to be the real person behind the figure of Tristan of Tristan and Isolde fame. Most frequently the inscription is in (often crudely executed) Roman capitals, while the later inscriptions may be in a version of 'Insular Script', which is really a book hand. On the earlier stones in Cornwall, but also to a small extent in Devon, the Latin script and text are also given in Irish in the ogham script. This is a script invented in Ireland, using groups of parallel lines to represent sounds. The inscription is usually placed on the edge of the stone.

In Northern Devon we know of two inscribed stones and there is anecdotal evidence of a third, now lost. If we like to reach across the Somerset border there is another which we might vicariously claim as a fourth. This stands on the edge of Exmoor above Winsford. The inscription reads simply CARATACI NEPUS, ie 'kinsman of Caratacus'. People like to associate this name with Caractacus, the British leader who defied the Roman invaders, but there is no reason for this. The name is simply an

The Cavudus stone in a garden near Caffyns Heanton.

early form of the Welsh name Caradoc. Moving back into Northern Devon, our best known local example stands in the garden of Six Acre Farm (SS700 483) in Lynton parish. Found in 1913 being used as a gate-post at Caffyns Cross, the stone bears the inscription CAVVDI FILIVS CIVILI(S), ie '(memorial of) Cavudus son of Civilis'. Possibly dating from the 6th century, the pair of names, the father's Latin, the son's Brittonic (modern welsh Cewydd), seems to represent a time when local society and culture were in transition. Found most recently (2012) at West Down is a somewhat later inscription rendered in insular script and containing the inscription GUERNGENI ('memorial of Guerngen'). The suggested date of this stone, late 8th or early 9th century, implies that Guerngen may have been one of the last members of a Brittonic elite in Northern Devon. The stone apparently spent the last 100 years or so built into a roadside boundary wall, which was demolished in 1997. Before being built into the wall it may have been located within or near the parish church. The third North Devon stone is reported by the Rev. Chanter in the late 19th century to have been built into the parapet of the bridge over the River Heddon at Parracombe. As the bridge was washed away in the flood of 1952, the stone may now be lying unrecognised somewhere between Parracombe and Heddons Mouth.

Finally, there are four more inscribed stones on Lundy. These are all from a walled graveyard associated with the remains of a medieval church dedicated to St Helen. The stones bear the inscriptions OPTIMI, POTITI, RESTEUTA(E) and TIGERNI. The first two represent Latin male names, the third is probably Brittonic and female. Optimus and Potitus are thought by Charles Thomas (1994, 166) to have been priests. All three are clearly Christian as the names are accompanied by a device showing a cross in a circle. The inscription on the fourth stone – actually the first to be discovered (in 1905) – may be a title rather than a name and means something like 'lord', possibly a 5th/6th century leader from North Devon.

Apart from these which appear to be grave-markers within a graveyard, many of the inscribed stones have been found in locations which suggest that their original purpose was not only to stand as a memorial, but also and probably equally to stake a family, tribal or dynastic claim to territory or – very importantly - to grazing rights. Certainly the Caratacus stone stands at the end of a track leading from Winsford onto the moor and the

Cavudus stone was found at or near the end of a route leading from Lynton onto Caffyns Heanton Down. It is possible that the stone recently found at West Down was similarly located on Fullabrook Down. Like others of its kind, it was probably removed from its original site and brought to the church, where its apparently Christian credentials would be honoured. (TG)

Note: The CAVUDUS stone may be viewed by arrangement with the owners of Six Acre Farm. The GUERNGEN stone is currently (2015) on display in the Museum of Barnstaple and North Devon.

Further Reading:

Thomas C 1994: *And Shall these Mute Stones Speak?* University of Wales Press.

Iron Age

The Iron Age is *probably* well represented in Northern Devon, but we cannot be definite about it, because so little excavation of potentially Iron Age sites has taken place. The hillforts and hillslope enclosures discussed under 'Hillforts' and 'Enclosures' probably represent Iron Age activity, but proof is lacking. Only the largely eroded Embury Beacon 'cliff castle' south of Hartland has received close archaeological attention which has produced dating material in the form of Iron Age pottery. The following therefore, is a general introduction to the Iron Age.

The smelting of iron requires the achievement of higher temperatures than the smelting of copper. The earliest metallurgists were not able to achieve such high temperatures, thus iron technology arrived later than that of copper and bronze. Named, like the Bronze Age, for its distinctive metal technology, the Iron Age in Britain is usually dated from around 700 BC, and is conventionally brought to a close with the Roman invasion of AD 43. For our purposes, the Iron Age represents the transition from prehistory to 'proto-history' the earliest period for which we have documentary records provided by Roman commentators.

While culturally the Iron Age is characterised by, on the one hand, beautifully executed art work in metal and correspondingly elegant pottery, and on the other hand by the construction of elaborate banked and ditched hilltop citadels, so-called hillforts, it is probably better represented by the ways in which the land was used. From this period we have evidence, in the south of England at least, of widespread farming settlements and communities with a highly productive farming regime. We don't really know what the hillforts were for – their elaborate earthworks were perhaps more for show than any real defensive purpose. However, at Danebury (Hampshire), the most extensively excavated hillfort, there is clear evidence of numerous round houses, workshops, a possible 'temple' and, most strikingly, large numbers of deep chalk-cut pits which were evidently used for the storing of grain. This was presumably produced by farmers in the surrounding landscape who must have carried their produce to the hillfort for storage. This would then see the community through to the next season. The fact that the Roman geographer Strabo records grain among Britain's exports means that the farming regime was producing a surplus.

The evidence of the hillforts suggests a strongly centralised and hierarchical tribal society. From Roman sources the names of the major tribes and of some of their rulers are known, and it is evident that before the Roman invasion of AD 43 the insular British elite were adopting Roman ways. From the trading 'emporium' at Hengistbury Head (Poole) there is evidence of the importing of wine and oil from the continent in exchange, presumably, for 'slaves, grain and hunting dogs' as recorded by Strabo. An additional and significant import from the continent was coinage. At first coins were brought from the continent, but by the 1st century BC they were being produced in Britain. Finds of hoards of gold 'staters' stamped with a conventional design of a stylised horse or a boar and, in later examples, with the head of a tribal leader and an inscription, an abbreviated form of his name, signal the accumulation of portable wealth. The coinage was probably not used in trade, but was rather used in a system of gift exchange among the elite.

Perhaps the best known Iron Age hillfort is Maiden Castle in Dorset. 'Multivallate' hillforts of this type are widespread in England. However, apart from Hembury hillfort near Honiton, the elaborate 'classic' hillfort is scarcely evident in Devon. Promontory forts or cliff castles such as Hillsborough (Ilfracombe) and Windhill (Lynmouth) are a different class of monument and not really comparable. The nearest thing to a classic hillfort might be Clovelly Dykes, but this multivallate structure with its truly massive ditches is different in too many ways to be grouped together with the hillforts of Wessex. Aside from these and described by some as hillforts are hilltop earthworks which might be seen as 'proto-hillforts' and in a different class entirely are the numerous ringworks known as hillslope enclosures ('rounds' in Cornwall) which are said to be of Iron Age origin and likely to be enclosed farmsteads in what was probably a predominantly pastoral society. (TG)

Limekilns

Disused limekilns are a distinctive feature of the Northern Devon coast, but especially the Taw and Torridge estuaries, where they might perhaps be mistaken for miniature castles, sometimes having quite elaborate crenellated tops, for example at Pillmouth, Halsannery on the banks of the Torridge (SS461 247). Northern Devon's soils are generally acidic and thus benefit from the application of alkaline materials. Beach sand containing shell fragments helps to reduce soil acidity and was traditionally carted from the beaches to spread on the land; the practice is commemorated in the Sandy Lanes found in coastal areas. However, progressively from the eighteenth century,

farmers took to applying lime. There are a few small beds of limestone in the Devonian rocks around Ilfracombe, Combe Martin and Challacombe and again in the lowest Carboniferous rocks in a band from Venn, just outside Barnstaple through to Stag's Head, east of Filleigh. These limestones were worked to feed a series of limekilns. However, the coal to burn the limestone had to be brought in by pack-horse or cart and the inland sites were at something of a disadvantage compared to the coastal sites where both coal and limestone could be brought in by ship. Along the valley of the East Lyn is a well built limekiln which must have been difficult of access and would certainly have presented dificulties in carting the product away.

Lime kilns at Bucks Mills. (Photo: North Devon AONB)

Most of the limestone burnt in Northern Devon's limekilns came from South Wales, principally Pembrokeshire and the Gower. Coal too came from South Wales, although some coal from the Forest of Dean was also used. Most land-owners seem to have wanted to have their own kiln which explains the sheer numbers around the coast. At Bucks Mills (SS35 23), for instance the western kiln provided lime for Woolsery and the impressive eastern kiln, with its inclined plane, supplied lime for Parkham.

Coal and limestone were brought in by ship to the beach, to

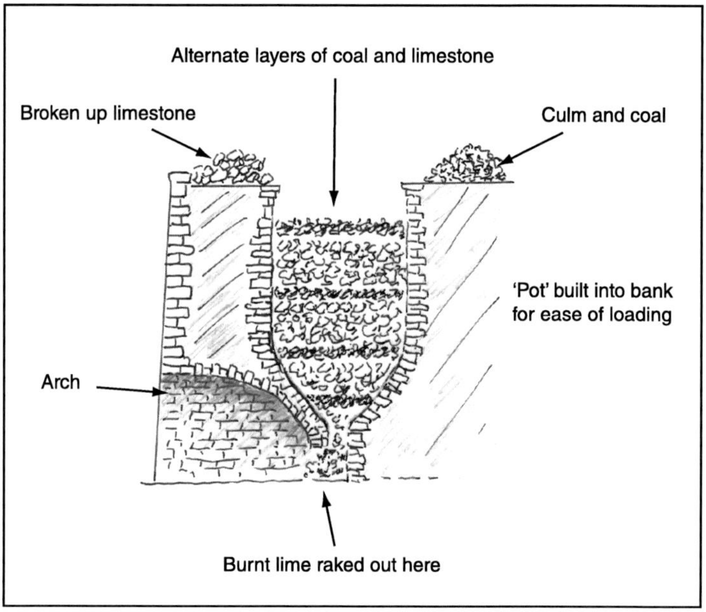

Sketched cross-section of a single-arched limekiln showing the principal features. Built into a bank, there might be several such side by side.

be unloaded between tides. Coal, being more valuable than limestone was unloaded directly into carts, but the limestone was often just dumped on the beach to be collected later. The entire year's supply of coal and limestone would be delivered during the summer and the kiln kept burning continuously from March until December. A typical kiln would take 8 tonnes of limestone and 2 tonnes of coal to yield 6 tonnes of quicklime and a variable amount of lime-ash, a mixture of coal ash and lime. The quicklime would be slaked in water before transport to farms. In the eighteenth and nineteenth centuries, about 3.5 tonnes of lime would be applied to each hectare if cereals were to be grown, but each application was reckoned to suffice for three years. There are roughly 170 kilns known in Northern Devon on 109 sites. Excellent surviving examples are those at Bucks Mills west (SS354 236), Bucks Mills east (SS356 236), Greencliff (SS404 269), Ashford Strand (SS522 349) and Heddons Mouth (SS655 497) all of these being visible from the North Devon coast path. Limer's Lane in Northam leads to a former limekiln which has been adapted for domestic residential purposes, while at Fremington Quay a complex of several large lime-kilns attests to the historically economic significance of this part of the Taw estuary. (JB)

Further reading:

Hughes B D (2006) *Rolle Canal and the North Devon Limestone Trade*. Bideford: Edward Gaskell.

Mansions

Although Devon had its share of major landed families, few were as opulent as those of other parts of the country and so the great houses are generally not a spectacular as those further to the east. Northern Devon contained the family seats of under half of the major Devon estates (defined as being over 10,000 acres – 4050 hectares) in 1873. Perhaps seven sites might qualify as 'grand houses' but there are many more gentlemen's country houses of more modest design. Two major houses no longer survive. Perhaps the greater loss is Dunsland House in Bradford parish (SS408 052). This largely Tudor house had been acquired by the National Trust and restoration was nearly completed when it was

Tawstock Court, a mansion in the Gothick style.

Castle Hill, Filleigh, Northern Devon's grandest mansion.

destroyed by fire in 1967. The other to have been lost is Stevenstone, in St Giles-in-the-Wood parish (SS527 194), which was the home of the Rolle family. Several houses were built here and the Library and Orangery of one, otherwise demolished in 1868, still survive, although the large Franco-Italian château style house designed by Charles Barry junior and built 1868-1872, has all gone. The Rolle estate was inherited in 1907 by Lord Clinton, who chose to live at his other houses and so sold Stevenstone. The house itself was offered for sale in lots for demolition by a succeeding owner but not finally demolished until the 1950s. The original Clinton house, Jacobean in style, was at Heanton Satchville in Petrockstow and was destroyed by fire in 1795. It was never rebuilt and a replacement house, also called Heanton Satchville, was built 4 kilometres to the east at Huish (SS533 111). It too was destroyed by fire in 1932 and rebuilt in a late seventeenth century style to designs by Sir Walter and Michael Tapper in 1937-8.

Northern Devon has two eighteenth century Gothick style houses, at Tawstock Court (SS558 299) and at Hartland Abbey

(SS241 249). The former was built by Sir Bouchier Wray with probable help from Sir John Sloane in the late 1780s. Hartland Abbey is a late eighteenth century remodelling of the remains of the Augustinian Abbey and a northern wing was constructed in 1862 to designs by Giles Gilbert Scott, also in a Gothic style. Arlington Court (SS 614 405) is a neo-classical house of 1820-3, with its plain exterior giving little clue to the far grander interior.

Probably the grandest of all Northern Devon's great houses is Castle Hill, Filleigh (SS671 285). It is Palladian in style and Hugh Fortescue, its builder, seems to have consulted Lord Burlington on its design. It commands its site and the road from Swimbridge to South Molton was deliberately moved and then made sinuous to show the house off to its greatest effect. The park was landscaped and the 'Castle' from which the house takes its name was constructed on the hill to the north in c1746. The eastern wing of the house was extensively remodelled in the mid nineteenth century, without changing the view of the house from the south. A major fire damaged the house in 1934 and it was restored to sustain its eighteenth century appearance. (JB)

Further reading:
Cherry B and Pevsner N 1989: *The Buildings of England: Devon.* London: Penguin.
Lauder R 2005 (revised edition): *Vanished Houses of North Devon.* Tiverton: North Devon Books.

Medieval

Use of the term 'medieval' can be variable. Older writers would probably reserve the term for the period from the Norman Conquest to the 16th century, referring to time before the Conquest as the Saxon period or even the Dark Ages. This latter term is now thankfully going out of use, though it may still occasionally be used as a short-hand for that obscure period between the end of Roman Britain and the establishment of the Anglo-Saxon kingdoms of Wessex, Mercia etcetera. Today archaeologists use the term medieval to cover the entire period from the immediate post-Roman 5th century up to the end of the reign of Henry VIII (1547), subdividing this long period of time into early medieval – say up to the 11th century – and later or 'high' medieval, 12th to mid-16th century. This basically arbitrary division is made meaningful in historical terms when we consider the early medieval period as comprising the coming of the English and the formation of England up to the coming of the Normans, and the later medieval period as embracing the development of Anglo-Norman society, the beginnings of what we recognise as English literature, the growth of towns, the invention of printing and, at its end, the Renaissance of learning and the Reformation.

In Devon the early medieval period does not fall quite so neatly into this simple scheme. It was not until the late 7th and early 8th century that Devon became part of the kingdom of Wessex. During the period of around 200 years in which the Germanic immigrants were settling into Britain and forming their kingdoms, West Somerset, Devon and Cornwall maintained their Brittonic (Celtic) character as the kingdom of Dumnonia. Of this post-Roman kingdom we know very little archaeologically. There is a certain amount of ceramic evidence indicating trade with the Mediterranean carried along the Atlantic seaboard and into the Bristol Channel, and there is evidence of the re-occupation of certain Iron Age hillforts. A number of stone memorials (see Inscribed Stones) point to the arrival of Christianity and, in the form of their inscriptions, hint at the gradual fading of Roman cultural memories, while new influences arrive from Ireland. There are documents that name certain Dumnonian rulers, and from a handful of written accounts it is evident that in this period Dumnonia and Brittany were closely tied. In this period the Celtic Church flourished and a variety of legendary saints emerged from South Wales to conduct their ministries in Northern Devon.

From the end of the 7th century Dumnonia became progressively absorbed into Wessex and with political change came changes of language, settlement patterns and landscape management as well as the fading of the Celtic church. With the exception of Exeter, pretty well all of our existing settlements originate in the period eighth to eleventh century.

As in the rest of England, the Norman Conquest brought a wholesale expropriation of the land by William's followers. The Domesday Book of 1086 provides us with a unique record of the Norman lords of Devon and the names and details of the manors which they acquired. Domesday Book tells us that Exeter, Totnes, Barnstaple and Lydford were boroughs, having in the late 9th century been turned into defensive burhs under the direction of King Alfred as part of his defence strategy against the Danes. It was not until the 12th to 14th centuries that numbers of ambitious lords attempted to turn their manors into boroughs with rent-paying burgesses and weekly markets. Some, such as Bideford and Torrington, succeeded in developing as urban centres, while there were numerous failures, among them Sheepwash, Rackenford, Hartland and Witheridge. Whatever earlier foundations there may have been, all of our existing parish churches were built in the later medieval period and are, with a few exceptions, the only buildings that survive from this time. Among the few secular survivals are Weare Gifford Hall, West Challacombe Manor (Combe Martin) and Bull House in Pilton, though many another building retains fragments of medieval work at its core.

The medieval period of roughly 1,000 years' duration is where the greater part of our understanding of the Northern Devon landscape begins. From this period emerges what we call the 'historic landscape' overlying the prehistoric 'relict landscape' with which it may or may not be discontinuous. The relationship between these two aspects of the landscape that surrounds us is a perennial topic of research. (TG)

Mesolithic

The Mesolithic ('Middle Stone Age') period is in many senses the last archaeological subdivision of the long Palaeolithic which term covers all human manufacturing cultures from the earliest simple chipped pebble tools around 2.5 million years ago up to around 12000 years ago. The term Mesolithic is used to identify the period after the ice of the last glaciation had retreated from Northern Europe and arctic tundra had been replaced by temperate deciduous forest. In north-western Europe the Mesolithic represents the period from roughly 10000 BC to about 4500 BC. The people of this time were hunter-gatherers, probably migrating seasonally to exploit whatever resources the varied post-glacial landscape might offer. Settlements were probably occupied seasonally: Star Carr in Yorkshire is the classic English Mesolithic site where seasonal occupation is evident. Much nearer to home, excavation in recent years at Hawkcombe Head near Porlock has revealed remains of what was probably a seasonally occupied Mesolithic site; and on the beach at Westward Ho! low tides reveal the remains of a 'kitchen midden ' ie. a food refuse dump, mainly shellfish, radio-carbon dated to the late Mesolithic.

Apart from rarely preserved habitation sites, our knowledge of the Mesolithic derives mainly from artefacts. Presented with an environment rich in resources, both plant and animal, marine and terrestrial, the people of this period developed a varied and specialised toolkit. Most particularly they developed a range of projectiles including arrows, spears and harpoons with barbed points. Where conditions favour the preservation of organic matter, we can see that, as well as stone, they worked in bone, wood and antler; in most circumstances however, it is only the stone that survives. Characteristic of the stone technology of the Mesolithic are what are known as microliths: small, carefully worked triangular or trapezoidal points designed to be glued with pitch to a shaft to form a row of barbs. They also made scrapers, burins, blades and axes. From stray individual finds to flint working scatters, examples of characteristic Mesolithic flint working are widely found in Northern Devon. The earliest, probably seasonal habitation site to be recognised was probably at Freshwater Gut on Baggy Point, reported on by M.Townshend-Hall in1865. Subsequent researchers have turned up prolific evidence of Mesolithic flint working on Baggy Point, concentrated on the south side of the headland from where in the early Mesolithic period you would have looked out over a coastal plain of woodland and wetland through which the Taw and the Torridge flowed to the sea. The beaches lying some way out in what is now the Bristol Channel would have provided raw materials in the form of flint pebbles which were carried back to the working sites to be flaked and shaped with exquisite care. Other recognised mesolithic working sites in the area tend to be similarly situated on high ground with a view of potential hunting grounds below.

Athough the people of the Mesolithic were hunter-gatherers, they probably began the transformation of the natural landscape for human purposes by fire and by cutting down trees with crudely shaped stone axes in order to create grassy glades where game might congregate. In this way they began the process of landscape change which characterises the succeeding period which we call the Neolithic. (TG)

Mills

The earliest references to mills in Northern Devon are to be found in Domesday Book (1086) although, in common with west and south Devon, they are few in number. A mill at Barnstaple, held by the Bishop of Coutances, returned 20 shillings and at Heanton Punchardon, on one of the many holdings of Baldwin the Sheriff, a mill was valued at 4 shillings. A mill at Lyn, on a manor held by William Cheever, had been newly built since the Conquest in 1066, the only mill to be so

Town Mill, Landkey. (Martin Watts)

recorded in Devon. The mill at Barnstaple, among the highest valued in the county at that time, was probably established in Anglo-Saxon times and may have been on or close to the site of the later Town Mills.

In the later Middle Ages references to mills become more frequent and many sites that were occupied by watermills into the 20th century have medieval origins. The primary use of water power was for grinding grain, wheat, barley and oats being the main cereals that were processed. Malt, an essential ingredient of brewing, was also milled. Medieval mills basically comprised a waterwheel, a pair of gears to change the direction of rotation from vertical to horizontal, and a pair of millstones. In the post-medieval period gearing was developed to enable more than one pair of stones to be driven by a single waterwheel, where the water supply was adequate. The type of waterwheel used - overshot, undershot or breast-shot - depended much on local topography.

Granite from Dartmoor was used for millstones and more expensive, better quality stones were imported. Welsh stones, of sandstone conglomerate, were imported into Barnstaple and French stones, the best for milling wheat to make fine flour, were widely used from at least the 18th century. In the late 19th century the use of millstones for grinding wheat for flour was superseded by the roller milling process. Some traditional watermills introduced the new technology, such as at North Molton Mill where a porcelain roller mill, now preserved at Hele Mill, Ilfracombe (SS535 475), was installed. At Weare Gifford on the river Torridge new roller plant driven by a water turbine was put in by miller John Fry in the 1880s. In the same period many watermills were still using more traditional waterwheels and machinery to drive millstones, such as at Plaistow Mill, Shirwell,

Overshot water wheel, Town Mill, Landkey. (Martin Watts)

which was rebuilt after a major fire in 1890.

The millwrights who built and maintained mills and machinery were formerly widespread, from local craftsmen to companies employing a number of men. The last large firm was Garnish and Lemon, based in Pilton, who made and installed waterwheels and other milling equipment in the late 19th and early 20th centuries. An example of their work can be seen at Hele Mill, Ilfracombe. They also installed a number of waterwheels on farms to drive threshing machines and other barn machinery, as at Wheel, Berrynarbor.

Another important and early use of waterwheels was to drive fulling stocks, for finishing cloth by felting the woven woollen fibres together. The process has left little in the way of physical remains other than some buildings, but the local term for fulling - tucking - survives in both place and personal names.

Windmills were always few in Devon, but there are the remains of a possible late-medieval tower mill on a prominent site overlooking the Estuary at Instow. There was also a tide mill at Instow in the late 18th century. At Bidna, Northam, there are fragmentary remains of a brick tower mill that was built on what appear to be foundations for the trestle of a post mill, an unusual and interesting survival. Other windmill sites can be located from place names and old maps.

Very few mills remain in working order, although Hele Mill near Ilfracombe has been restored and can be seen working, albeit driven by a diesel engine. Where mill wheels survive they are usually locked and serve as ornament. A feature that frequently does survive in a 'working'state is the mill leat, a canalised stream drawn off a natural watercourse and leading to the mill where the concentrated and controllable stream provided the force to turn the wheel. (MW)

Further reading:

Minchinton W 1977: *Windmills of Devon*, Exeter Industrial Archaeology Group, Exeter

Thorpe J (ed). 1989: *North Devon Watermills.* North Devon Archaeological Society, Barnstaple
University of the Third Age. 1994: *Watermills in North Devon* 1994

Neolithic

The Neolithic or new Stone Age is the term used by archaeologists to designate that period when the hunters and gatherers of the Mesolithic (Middle Stone Age) began to farm and to develop permanent settlements. As the term suggests, the durable evidence of this period is still dominated by stone, but the change of life-style demonstrated by other evidence represents such a profound development in human history that it has been described as the 'Neolithic revolution'. The shift away from hunting and gathering began in the area of the Middle East known as the 'Fertile Crescent' some time around 10000 years ago. Over the following millennia the practice of farming spread slowly across Europe, both by colonisation and by the dissemination of ideas, arriving in Britain around 4000 BC. Recent examination of the drowned landscape of the Solent between the mainland and the Isle of Wight has turned up evidence of cultivated grains (the primitive wheats emmer and einkorn) in a Mesolithic context. This material is thought to represent transcontinental trade rather than an earlier beginning of the British Neolithic, though trade in foodstuffs might be seen as a precursor to the growing of grain in Britain.

The security of permanent settlement and an assured food supply, even a surplus, provided the context in which well defined cultures began to flourish. Out of this period come the earliest pottery, art (leaving aside the cave art of the European Palaeolithic) and sculpture, complex social organisation and religious practices, writing and, unfortunately, warfare. In Britain this is the period in which ritual structures such as Avebury and Stonehenge have their beginning. Burial was typically in long barrows which housed the bones of multiple individuals whose bodies had been exposed in open mortuary enclosures where the flesh was removed by natural processes. Stone technology became more sophisticated, typical products of the time being polished stone axes and a variety of specialised arrow-heads. Pottery production flourished. Neolithic houses tended to be rectangular, as revealed by the excavation of the earliest known Neolithic settlement in Britain at Kingsmead Quarry near Windsor and the very recent discovery of a collection of Neolithic houses near Heathrow. Settlement reached as far north as the Orkneys where the stone built houses of Skara Brae represent the best preserved prehistoric settlement in Western Europe.

In Northern Devon evidence of this period is sparse, being represented mainly by scattered finds of characteristic leaf-shaped arrow-heads and polished stone axes, though predominantly of the probably non-utilitarian greenstone variety (see Axes). From Kentisbury Down comes a fine polished discoidal flint knife. The Mesolithic site at Freshwater Gut on Baggy Point excavated by M. Townshend-Hall in the 1860s produced a small number of sherds of crude pottery which appears to be Neolithic (suggesting therefore some sort of Mesolithic/Neolithic transition?). Both the knife and the pottery are to be seen in the Museum of Barnstaple and North Devon. We have no clear dating evidence for the various stone rows, settings, standing stones and circles that are found on Exmoor: They may be Neolithic, as may what appears to be a mortuary enclosure near Chapman Barrows. In fact the Neolithic of Northern Devon is an obscure period awaiting the results of current and future research. (TG)

Norman Castles

Following the defeat of the English at the Battle of Hastings in 1066, the Norman conqueror William the Bastard wasted no time in subduing a resentful population. One of the abiding memorials of this period is the number of Norman castles that survive in the landscape. Typically the castle of the 11th/12th century period is of the 'motte and bailey' variety. These were not the great stone castles of the later Middle Ages, but rapidly erected bases for soldiery led by a powerful lord. A castle of this period usually consisted of an enclosure called a bailey containing living quarters, stables, workshops and armoury, the whole surrounded by a rampart with an outer moat. There might often be an inner and an outer bailey. The bailey was dominated by a large mound called the motte on which stood a tower built first of wood, often later rebuilt in stone. On either side of the tower were 'wing walls' running down either side of the motte. Well preserved examples – beyond our area – are the castles at Totnes and Launceston.

In Northern Devon we have one very well preserved example. Most clearly displaying the form of the motte and bailey and largely intact is Holwell Castle at Parracombe (SS670 446). Created on a spur of land, the motte mound is surrounded by a ditch and has traces of wing walls. Survey within the bailey has suggested the presence of a hall, but there are at present no clear traces of other buildings. The castle is located on private land (but is visible from the parish churchyard) a short distance from the centre of the present village of Parracombe, which means that it is dominated by higher ground in almost all directions, not at all a defensive position. So why is it here? It has been suggested that it controls a crossing point on the River Heddon, but this seems insufficient reason to go to so much effort. At present its existence here remains a mystery, but probably has more to do with local power relationships than any national purpose.

Less well preserved, but dominant in its context is the castle mound beside Barnstaple Library. Built at the point where the River Yeo flows into the Taw, its purpose would have been to control movement on the rivers and to dominate the already

Holwell Castle, Parracombe: the very well preserved earthworks of a motte-and-bailey castle. (Photo: Jeremy Holtom)

well established borough of Barnstaple. From Castle Green a spiral path will take you to the top where a level platform once held the 'donjon', at first a wooden tower, later a stone-built keep. The castle was probably built between 1071 and 1086, in the process destroying a Saxon graveyard and apparently 23 houses (Domesday Book). Around 1100 it came into the possession of Judhel of Totnes. There was an inner bailey at the north-west, where now is Castle Green and probably an outer bailey on the south-east encompassing what is now the Cattle Market carpark. By order of the Sheriff of Devon in 1228 the walls were reduced in height and by the end of the 13th century the castle was already ruinous. When Leland visited in 1540 he found only a few walls standing. There is now nothing left to see.

Smaller castles like that at Parracombe existed at Loxhore – Castle Roborough (SS620 377), Shebbear (SS430 127) and Milton Damerel (SS397 126). Castle Roborough near Loxhore is quite impressive and easily accessible as it is situated beside a public footpath. Actually in Mid Devon, but well worth a look is a very impressive example – now cleared of trees – which is publicly accessible in Heywood Wood, Eggesford at SS679 126. (TG)

Further Reading:

Creighton O and Higham R 2003: *Medieval Castles*, Shire Books.

Barker P and Higham R 1994: *Timber Castles*, University of Exeter Press, Exeter.

Miles T 1987: The Excavation of a Saxon Cemetery and Part of the Norman Castle at North Walk, Barnstaple, in *Proceedings of the Devon Archaeological Society*, Vol.44.

Ores and Mines

Ores, metallic or other minerals present in sufficient quantities to be profitably extracted and processed, have probably been worked in the north of Devon since the late prehistoric periods although hard evidence is not available until the Roman occupation period. Iron, manganese, copper, lead and silver have all been mined and, apart from manganese, all have been processed through to smelting on site at certain periods during the last two thousand years. Gold-bearing deposits have also been worked at North Molton although they were hardly profitable.

Iron ores were worked across the north from Little Hangman at Combe Martin to Molland. On either side of the River Bray, at Charles and at Brayford, iron was been smelted from at least the second century AD but the exact source of the ores used there is unknown as no extraction sites for that period have been identified. There are, however, significant iron deposits in the area from Charles across to North Molton, which are known to have been worked from at least the 18th century onwards at sites such as Barton Pits (SS724 320) and Crowbarn Wood (SS738 318).

A large mass of tap-slag from the Roman iron-working site at Brayford. (Centimetre scale)

There were ferruarios (iron workers) at North Molton in 1086, but again, the exact location of the iron ores they worked is, as yet, unknown. The peak in iron ore production came in the second part of the 19th century when, after the development of the Bessemer process for steel production, there was a demand for iron ores rich in manganese. By the 1870s mines had been opened up around Georgeham, at Molland and around Heasley Mill (North Molton). The Florence Mine (SS751 319) and the workings in Crowbarn Wood were linked to the main line railway at South Molton by a narrow gauge tramway, the earthworks for which can still be traced down the Mole valley.

There was a similar revival in the mining of manganese ores in the late 19th century, mines such as that at Fullabrook (SS515 398) near Braunton, with its water-powered crushing mill, were opened up to supply not only the steel industry but increased demand for the mineral as a deoxiding agent across the industrial sector. This, and other mines in the north, were probably also worked from the 18th century when Devon was the major supplier of the manganese ores used in the English glass industry.

Copper in Northern Devon has a medieval pedigree with a

mine, probably the Bampfylde Mine (SS737 327) at North Molton, documented in the mid-14th century. Field evidence, in the form of slag with entrapped charcoal dates copper smelting on the Bampfylde site to the late 15th century. From the 1690s, through to the mid 18th century Northern Devon was at the forefront of an expanding copper industry with Bampfylde, and mines at East Buckland (SS619 318) and Molland (Bremley, SS818 283 - and Gourt, SS823 283), contributing to the shipment of copper ores coastwise to smelters in Bristol and the Wye Valley. The mine at Bampfylde and those at Molland contined to be worked intermittently through to the second part of the 19th century, and some significant earthworks and structures survive on all those sites. Bampfylde and the Britannia Mine to the north (SS745 335) were the site of attempts, in the 1840s and 50s, at large scale working of the gold found in association with the copper deposits. Those operations were not an economic success but, on the former site, there are surviving remains of structures associated with the amalgamation techniques (Berdan pans) employed.

The working of lead ores, and the extraction of the silver they held, has a similar medieval origin. Silver mines at Combe Martin were opened in 1292 and worked briefly under Crown management before they were abandoned in favour of those at Bere Ferrers in south Devon. The Combe Martin mines were subsequently leased to entrepreneurial interests and worked intermittently through to the 16th century, as were those at Brushford, near Dulverton, in the north-east. It was not until the late 16th century, with the discovery of new deposits, that the Combe Martin mines came to be significant producers. Evidence, in the form of residues from smelting and refining, survives from this period in the centre of the village along with subterranean features under Mine Tenement (SS588 464). From the 17th century onwards attempts to de-water the mines and work them below the water table continued, including the

A hand cut medieval / post-medieval working, now partially filled with later spoil, at Combe Martin (half metre scale bar). (Peter Claughton)

driving of a deep drainage adit from the Umber, west of the Pack of Cards, up to the workings under Mine Tenement. Pumping using water-wheels was tried in the early 19th century but it was not until mid-century and the application of steam power that the mines were worked in depth. Elements of the houses for the beam pumping engines survive at Mine Tenement (Williams Shaft of the Old Combe Martin Mine) and at Knap Down (SS597 466). The lead ores were smelted and silver extracted at the smelter on the site now occupied by Loverings Garage (SS578 471) where the walls of the building and evidence for the flue survive. Earthworks also survive from other small 19th century lead mines across the north of Devon, notably at

Yarnscombe (SS543 244), East Combe (SS608 296) near Swimbridge, Combe Martin Consols (SS625 465) at Trentishoe, and at Parracombe (SS667 449).

Economic working of ores in Northern Devon ceased in the late 19th century with falling metal prices. Attempts were made to reopen some mines, notably at the Florence Iron Mine during the Second World War where some evidence survives, and prospecting was carried out with a view to reworking copper at North Molton in the 1970s. There is the possibility of further, hidden lead-silver deposits at Combe Martin but the likelihood that they would prove economically or environmentally viable is currently slim. (PC)

Further reading:

Atkinson M (ed) 1997 *Exmoor's Industrial Archaeology*, Tiverton: Exmoor Books

Claughton P 2004 *The Combe Martin Mines, 3rd edn*, Combe Martin Local History Group

Claughton P, Paynter S and Dunkerley T 2005 *Further work on lead smelting at Combe Martin, Devon*, www.people.exeter.ac.uk/pfclaugh/mhinf/Lead_si.pdf

Rippon S, Claughton P and Smart C 2009 *Mining in a Medieval Landscape: the Royal Silver Mines of the Tamar Valley*, Exeter: University of Exeter Press, particularly Chapter 2

Pipes, Clay

In 1975 a ground-breaking book "Clay Pipes for the Archaeologist" listed just one pipemaker from Northern Devon: William Short of Bideford, a nineteenth century practitioner. In the intervening time considerable advances have been made in our knowledge of an industry that must have thrived in the area given the supply of pipe clay at Peters Marland and the export market facilitated by the ports of Barnstaple and Bideford.

In 1985, Alison Grant and David Jemmett, having scoured

documentary sources such as port books and parish registers (as well as looking at excavated material), produced extensive lists of Bideford and Barnstaple pipemakers from the early 1600s to the late 1800s.

In 1986 and 1988, the North Devon District Rescue Archaeology Unit produced reports on two kiln sites in Barnstaple. The earliest, at Potters Lane, produced kiln furniture and pipes dated between 1610 and1630. The second, at Alexandra Road, was the site of the Seldon factory which produced fine quality clay pipes from 1857 to 1865. As well as kiln debris, 1,500 complete bowls and 40,000 stem fragments were found, giving some idea of the scale of production. Commercial archaeology in the 21st century has unearthed Seldon pipes at Combe Martin, Totnes, Charles and Brayford amongst other places. The initials 'JS' are on either side of the spur.

In 2005, part of a wall in Appledore collapsed, revealing four bowls and 12 stem fragments which had been mixed with the mortar to block in a window. These were early examples, suggesting deposition between 1620 and 1650. Two of the bowls are associated with Barnstaple pipemakers: Tamsin Garland and Peter Stephens. Were the pipes a seaman's 'share' of an export order? Another commonly found Barnstaple pipe is that with the 'Barum' mark on the flat-heeled spurs of bowls. As well as being widespread in Northern Devon, these bowls have turned up in Plymouth in a deposit sealed c.1740, in Crediton, in Worcester and as far afield as Newfoundland. Grant and Jemmet give them a broad date range of 1660 -1740.

Most recently, research in Northern Devon is being focussed on the Merton area where a number of pipemakers are coming to light. This is not unexpected given the proximity to the source of white clay at Peters Marland (used also in the 19th century for making the characteristic Northern Devon Marland brick.)

For the archaeologist, clay pipes are invaluable as a dating tool in post-medieval contexts. Sometimes they can date a context

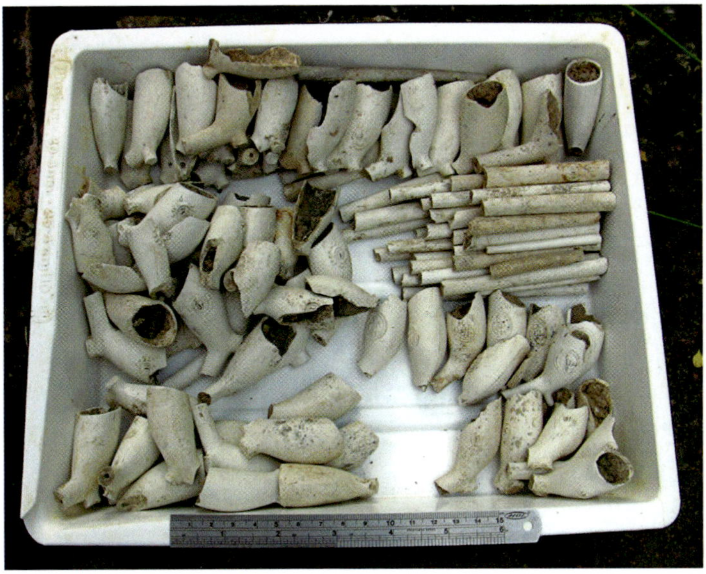

A collection of pipe bowls and stems from a manufacturing site near Merton. (Chris Preece)

very precisely (as in the case of the Seldon pipes due to their short lifespan) but usually a date range between twenty and forty years is the norm.

In order to assign a date and origin, the name or the initials of the maker are an important identifier. As a general rule, the following criteria help with dating. In the 17th century names or initials were often stamped on the base of a flat heeled spur. In the 18th century, particularly in the West Country, moulded marks on the side of bowls sometimes bore the maker's mark. In the nineteenth century a common practice was for the initial of the Christian name to be on the left of the spur (looking from stem to bowl) and the surname on the right. So a nineteenth century bowl with the initials WS found locally would probably have originated in Bideford at the hands of William Short. He is listed as a pipemaker in Meddon Street in 1856.

Sometimes however, there are no name identifiers and in this case the form is the only clue to date. Basically, the earliest bowls are smaller and the angle of stem to bowl is greater. The flat heeled spur was superseded by a more pointed spur in the first half of the eighteenth century. At this time, incised or stamped decoration of stems and bowls became more widespread with moulded or relief decoration developing in the second half of the eighteenth century and becoming the norm in the nineteenth century. Most experts can date the form of the bowl to within 40 years or so based on typologies constructed over time.

These days there are only a handful of pipemakers left in the UK. One of the most accomplished, Heather Coleman, lives and works in Devon and produces fine quality pipes for enthusiasts, re-enactors and thespians. (CP)

Further Reading:

Blanchard L 1988: *Archaeology in North Devon* 1987-8. North Devon District Council Rescue Archaeology Unit.

Grant A and Jemmett D 1985: Pipes and Pipemaking in North Devon, in Davey, P.J. (ed) *The Archaeology of the Clay Tobacco pipe* IX BAR 146.

Preece C and Thompson P 2009: A Cache of early Clay Pipes from Appledore, in *Proceedings of the Devon Archaeological Society* 67.

Terry R 1989: *The Barnstaple Clay Tobacco Pipe factory* (NDDC Rescue Archaeology Unit).

www.dawnmist.org (Heather Coleman's website)

Place-names

The majority of the place-names with which we are familiar were coined by people living in and working the landscape at least a millennium ago. To most people today their meaning is obscure and is rarely given a thought, but to those who first spoke them they represented present reality. Thus, for a place-name specialist they present a partial view of the way our ancestors perceived the landscape and the impact that they had upon it. Therefore just as physical archaeology is built on the material record, so a kind of linguistic archaeology can be developed from the place-name record.

The earliest stratum of place-names in Devon comprises – either wholly or partially – terms from the Brittonic speech of Dumnonia. Purely Brittonic are Landkey (holy place of St Kea), Landcross (holy place in the marsh), Croyde (cradle), Charles (hall on the rock) and Trellick (farm of a person called Felec) – probably also Clovelly (earthwork associated with Fele(c)?). So too are the river names Taw and Torridge. Taw means 'the silent one' and Torridge 'the turbulent one'! Partly Brittonic are Penhill, Molland, Kentisbury, Rosedown, Nympton and a few others. Nympton contains the Brittonic term *nemeton* 'sacred grove or wood'. For an area which was absorbed into Saxon Wessex relatively late (7th-8th century) the traces of Brittonic nomenclature are puzzlingly few.

Trellick, near Hartland, one of three place-names in Devon that display the 'Tre-' prefix, otherwise now confined to Cornwall.

With the spread of West Saxon rule into Dumnonia - now Devon - came, it appears, radical change in land management and the settlement pattern. Thus the vast majority of our place-names stem from this transitional period and reflect the new regime and the course of landscape change.

Place-name scholars broadly divide place-names into two types: topographic and habitative. Topographic place-names refer to features of the landscape such as hills and valleys, rivers, streams, springs etc – features that were reference points for finding your wayabout. Examples in our area might be Shirwell (clear spring), Challacombe (cold valley), Roborough (rough hill), Horwood (grey wood), Bideford (Bidda's ford) and so on. The last of this short list represents a landscape feature associated with a named person, a type of name which is common in our area.

The names with the greatest potential to provide clues to landscape evolution are the so-called habitative names, that is those which refer to settlements. Principally these end in –ton, -worthy, -ham and –cott. The element ton from Old English tūn, has a chequered history: originally signifying fence or hedge, it evolved to embrace enclosure, estate, manor, farmstead, settlement and ultimately became the modern English word 'town'. Place-names which, in general, combine a river name or a feature of the landscape with -ton, such as Tawton, Torrington, Molton, Crediton, Cullompton (and quite probably Braunton) are thought to represent the centres of large estates with very early, probably pre-English origins. Such large estate centres would have had dependent settlements exploiting the resources of the land and paying tribute to the centre.

The changes that came with the West-Saxon take-over seem to have involved a shift from enclosed settlements to open settlements with attached field-systems. This change represented the adoption of a system of 'convertible husbandry', an infield-outfield system (see 'Field Systems'). The intensively cultivated infield would be enclosed and might be called a 'worthy', which was originally another term for enclosure. The process of enclosing more land for cultivation, may have also been expressed through the element 'ham'. This term, from Old English *hamm* and related to the word 'hem', was generally used for land partly surrounded by water, but especially in the Southwest came to be used for land taken in and enclosed from open downland or moor. So ultimately 'ton',' worthy' and 'ham' all represent the process of enclosure.

Within the short list presented above, -cott is heavily represented in Northern Devon, but hardly at all in South Devon, and is the most difficult to pin down. It is fairly obvious that the 'cotts' were minor settlements, possibly at the bottom of the hierarchy, but what exactly they represent is not clear. In the beginning they may have been seasonal settlements related to summer grazing, but they obviously did not stay that way. Before the Conquest two of them in our area, Alverdiscott and Tetcott, became manorial centres, presumably through the division of larger estates, lowly elements within which were raised high

During the early medieval period the feudal system of control was evolving, with power becoming distributed from the King

Ford, ham and worthy gathered together on a road sign. Meddon is another topographic name formed with –don ('Down').

downwards through dependent lords or thegns whose service was ensured through grants of land. This process is probably reflected in the numerous '-ington' names such as Fremington, Atherington, Alwington, (but not Torrington). In these a personal name is attached to 'ton' by the element –ing- , thus identifying lesser lords called Fremma, Aethelheare and Alwe (a woman, which is unusual) with the land granted to them. These names probably arose quite late in the Saxon period. Some of the richer estates, which were retained by the King as his personal fief, might become divided through grants to the Church, thus we have Kings Nympton and Bishops Nympton.

William the Conqueror was no less concerned to ensure loyalty, and having dispossessed Saxon lords, handed the land to his Norman followers. His successors did likewise and so we have double-barrelled place-names such as Heanton Punchardon , Milton Damerel, Ashreigney and Bratton Fleming, each of which comprises an Anglo-Saxon term coupled with the name of a Norman-French lord (de Ponte Cardonis or Ponchardon, de Albamarla, Regny and le Flameng). Otherwise the Norman-French influence on our place-names is minimal, restricted in our area to Meshaw originating as Norman French *mal-essart* 'unfertile clearing', though later influenced by the English term 'shaw', a small wood.

Finally, Northern Devon has one place-name which is of definite Norse (Viking) origin, namely Lundy, meaning 'puffin island'. We assume that it had an earlier Brittonic name.

These are just a few pointers in what is a very broad topic with the potential to tell us a great deal about the development of our landscape. (TG}

Further Reading:

Gelling M 1988: *Signposts to the Past: Place-Names and the History of England*, Chichester.

Gelling M and Cole A 2000: *The Landscape of Place-Names*, Lincoln.

Gover J, Mawer A and Stenton F 1931: *The Place-names of Devon, Part 1*, Cambridge.

Pottery

Pottery is the commonest artefact found in the soil. It is also the earliest material we humans made by transforming, by fire, a natural substance, clay, into an entirely different and very resilient artefact, pottery. The systematic recovery, plotting, recording and identification of sherds of pottery is often the key to understanding the development of human activity in an area, whether it is gathered during field- or shoreline- walking, site-watching, test pitting, full archaeological excavation or a combination of these techniques. Two words of warning: first, we like to think we can pick up a sherd of pottery and ascribe a date to it. It is possible sometimes, and more often with a little help from others. The more you look at archaeological collections and talk them over with others, the more competent you will become in recognising fabrics (the material the pottery is made of) and forms (the shapes of pots particular to their age and designed use). Second, Northern Devon is open to the waterways and seas of the west of the British Isles, Ireland and the Atlantic seaboard, both west and east, as well as its local river systems and overland routes. Pottery found here is not all made here, but reflects from the earliest times these widespread contacts.

Pottery was first used in this part of the world in the Neolithic period and is associated with a more settled lifestyle. It was used for both domestic purposes, cooking, storage and so forth, as well as accompanying or even containing the dead. It is all hand-made from clay containing quantities of added materials, such as shell and grits to make the ware more robust, and can have very sophisticated decoration usually inscribed or impressed. Pottery produced on a widespread industrial scale by throwing on a wheel and firing in a kiln was introduced here in the Roman period. The range of forms and types of pottery used was enormous, some of it finding its way here as containers for goods such as olive oil. So far there has been no hint that any pottery of this date was made in Northern Devon, though quantities of Roman pottery have been found in the excavation of Romano-British iron working sites near Brayford. In the immediate post-Roman period, various types of late Roman wares continued to be imported. Finds are sparse but distinctive.

Then in this part of the world there is a gap. Pottery seems to have gone out of use in favour of other materials. In about the tenth/eleventh century pottery is again found, the commonest form being the hand-built plain open-mouthed jar with sagging base. This was used for cooking, storage and possibly many other purposes. These vessels are also made of clay with much additional material to ensure the ware can withstand the shock of being put on a fire. Waste from making these was found with a late 13th-century kiln near the site of the new library in Barnstaple. Sherds of such pottery are often found in fields and gardens of Northern Devon and are typically thin, salmon pink and gritty. In the twelfth century Bristol started making jugs at Ham Green to the west of that city. These are hand-built,. In the following century finer wheel-thrown jugs were made there and at other centres such as Llandaff and were traded along the

A reconstructed kiln from Potter's Lane in the Museum of Barnstaple and North Devon.

Severn Estuary. By the fourteenth century, there is evidence of a local industry making similar jugs in a distinctive mica-rich clay.

When Northern Devon came into its own as a major pottery making centre in the late sixteenth/seventeenth century, it was part of that remarkable transition from the medieval world to the post-medieval. Impressive evidence of this transitional period came to light in late 2012 when quantities of sixteenth century pottery waste were excavated behind the old Exeter Inn in Litchdon Street in Barnstaple. The completely new extensive range of wares were all in red earthenware and sometimes tempered, particularly in the larger more robust forms, with crushed granite grits dredged from the estuary. Archaeological evidence for its making has been published from Great Torrington, Bideford and Barnstaple in the form of waste pottery and discarded kiln furniture from firing. In Potters Lane, Barnstaple, three kilns of this period were excavated, one of which was lifted, is preserved and can be seen partially reconstructed in the Museum of Barnstaple and North Devon. Best known are the more decorative forms of harvest jugs, cups and dishes where the red body has been overlaid with a white slip (liquid clay) and decoration, often extremely elaborate, scratched or cut though the slip to expose the body underneath – a technique known as sgraffito. In England this technique was at first peculiar to the potteries centred on North Devon and Somerset. And these were the wares that excited the attention of C Malcolm Watkins of the Smithsonian Institution in the USA when he recognised finds of this distinctive pottery in early European settlements along the eastern seaboard of what is now the United States of America. In the late nineteenth century it

A selection of North Devon pottery: Back left, a 14th century jug, back right, a clay fire-dog, front left, a 17th century sgraffito ware plate, centre, a post-medieval cup or bowl recovered from the Taw.

also inspired local potters like George Fishley, William Baron and Charles Brannam. Less common were those sixteenth/seventeenth-century wares decorated with trailed white slip patterns.

The bulk of post-medieval production was domestic wares for food storage and cooking. Usually this was glazed inside with a plain green lead glaze and sometimes had a band of white slip round the rim. The pancheon, a large deep bowl made of heavily gritted clay and used for scalding clotted cream, hence often found with burn marks on the base, was produced over a period of four hundred years virtually unchanged. As late as the second half of the twentieth century Brannams could still produce a catalogue advertising under the brand of Ye Olde Devon Cottage Ware the following forms – butter pot with cover, pitcher, bread pan, yellow top pitcher, sugar pot, salter, brown pot with cover, jam pot, butter pot, yellow pan, barm jar, poultry and pigeon feeder, flower pot 2 inch to 12 inch sizes, pipkin, cream pot, pigeon meat pan, pan, colander, 15 inch stein, baking dish and soap pan. On the Brannams site one 'bottle' kiln survives.

One other form, which was made right the way through to the twentieth century to be described by William Fishley Holland, was the cloam oven. These are large hand-built objects made of heavily gritted clay and destined to be built into the side of an open fire-place. Some other forms like the chafing dish fell out of fashion and do not seem to survive long into the eighteenth century and products such as tiles with raised decoration do not seem to have been made much after 1750.

In the eighteenth century local wares came under increasing pressure from finer wares from centres like Bristol with products like Delftwares (tin-glazed earthenwares), yellow slipwares and stonewares and later in the century, from the growing flood of creamwares from Bristol and Staffordshire. The revival of North Devon slipware hardly registers in the archaeological record. With the closure of Brannams pottery, industrial production in North Devon ceased. We are left with a first-hand portrait of

The ceramically decorated entrance arch to the former Brannam's pottery in Litchdon Street, built in 1886.

how many of the potteries functioned in the autobiography of William Fishley Holland and more generally in the beautifully illustrated account compiled by Andrew McGarva. The most substantial evidence survives in the excellent reference collections of the Museum of Barnstaple and North Devon. (DD)

Further reading:

Allan J, Horner B & Langman G (2005) 'Seventeenth- and eighteenth-century pottery waste from the Stella Maris Convent

School Site, Bideford', *Proceedings of the Devon Archaeological Society* 63, 167-203.
Allan J, Cramp C, & Horner B (2007) 'The post-medieval pottery at Castle Hill, Great Torrington, North Devon', *Proceedings of the Devon Archaeological Society* 68, 135-181.
Fishley Holland W (1958) *Fifty Years a Potter.* Tring: Pottery Quarterly.
Grant, A (2005) *North Devon Pottery.* Appledore: Edward Gaskell Publishing.

Quays and maritime trade

Northern Devon has a coastline of some 85 kilometres and much evidence of its importance in the life of the region. Archaeologists and historians wonder if the Roman fleet based in the Bristol Channel in the first century AD might have used the Taw or Torridge estuaries, but no evidence has been found, as perhaps the facilities necessary were slight and built of wood which has not survived. Indeed, there is little physical as opposed to documentary evidence of ships and shipping until the sixteenth century and it must be remembered that even late into

Fremington Quay and the railway to Bideford, about 1960.

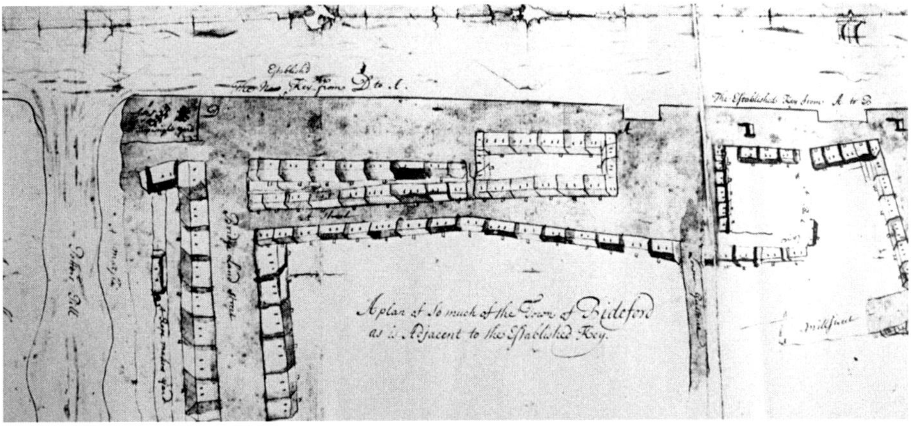

An 18th century plan of Bideford Quay. The inscription reads: *'A plan of so much of the Town of Bideford as is adjacent to the Established Key'.* (NDRO)

the nineteenth century, coastal ketches would come onto sand and shingle beaches at places like Hele Bay (SS535 479) near Ilfracombe, Combe Martin (SS575 473) and Greencliff in Abbotsham (SS285 272) to unload cargoes of coal, limestone and general merchandise. So the medieval port facilities of Barnstaple and Bideford may have been little more than the estuarine shore. Both Barnstaple and Bideford had stone quays in the sixteenth century and the extensions to the quay at Bideford in 1663, 1693 and by 1717 are commemorated by plaques set into the pavement. The various bouts of widening of the quay by some 20 metres are not as obvious, except by reference to mid nineteenth century photographs. Both Barnstaple and Bideford enjoyed considerable prosperity in the seventeenth and eighteenth centuries from trans-Atlantic trade exporting pottery and importing tobacco and above all from catching and trading cod from Newfoundland to the Mediterranean. Barnstaple's Great and Little Quays now lie beneath the gardens between Bridge Chambers and Queen Anne's Walk. The port facilities in Barnstaple were completely transformed in the 1870s following the construction of the railway to Ilfracombe. The railway itself cut the old quays off from the river and in compensation, Castle Quay was built further downstream but no rail sidings ever ran on it. Rolle Quay occupies the north bank of the river Yeo and was given a rail siding. The Yeo was entered via a rail swing bridge at its confluence with the Taw. A more modern swing bridge has been provided for the few yachts that now use the river. The railways also helped to create a new port at Fremington Quay (SS516 333), which had extensive sidings and was used for nearly a century to export ball-clay from Peters Marland. The quay itself survives, but is no longer in use.

In the eighteenth and nineteenth centuries there was considerable barge traffic on the Taw and Torridge and their principal tidal tributaries. A quay survives at Pilton (SS556 338) on the Barnstaple Yeo, whilst stakes can be seen protruding from the mud on the Bideford Yeo to enable barges to make their way up as far as Heale Mill bridge (SS454 235). The Torridge itself was navigable as far as Weare Gifford (SS470 221) and the Taw to Bishops Tawton (SS 565 363) where quays can still be seen. The river Caen was navigable as far as Wrafton but navigation was greatly improved in 1853-7 as part of the reclamation of Horsey Island and in 1870, a new quay was built at Vellator (SS485 355), which became the home for the

The Kathleen and May and the Oldenburg at Bideford Quay in 2014.

Ilfracombe's natural harbour.

Braunton fleet of schooners and ketches. Fremington Pill was navigable to Muddlebridge (SS522 325) so much of the clay used in Barnstaple's potteries arrived from here by barge and Fremington Pill itself remained accessible when the railway was built, as a swing bridge was initially provided.

Bucks Mills, Clovelly and Hartland all had quays constructed in the late sixteenth century. Only that at Clovelly survives (SS319 249), the others having succumbed to storms, with Hartland Quay finally disappearing in a great storm in October 1896. Clovelly's pier shows what the others were like. At both Hartland Quay (SS223 248) and Bucks Mills (SS354 237), some of the very largest boulders used as foundation stones can still be seen, although they are far more obvious at Hartland.

Ilfracombe is rather different from the other ports in Northern Devon. It has a natural harbour and has had both quays and a pier built to improve it. The present stone quay was built in 1760 and enlarged in 1824-9 and this protects a sizeable area, which, however, dries out completely at low tide. As steamers came to occupy a more important place in the maritime traffic of the Bristol Channel in the last part of the nineteenth century, a steamer pier was constructed in 1873 that allowed vessels to embark and disembark passengers at any state of the tide. The steamer pier itself was reconstructed after World War II and then again in recent years.

A characteristic of English seaside resorts is the pier, usually constructed of wrought iron, and as important as a promenade or centre of entertainment as for shipping. Northern Devon boasted two short-lived Victorian pleasure piers, although neither could be claimed as classic exemplars. In 1895-7, a pier was constructed at Woody Bay (SS677 492) as part of the project to develop a resort there. The pier was originally intended to be accessible to steamers at all states of the tide, but the tidal range here is as much as 11 metres on springs and the pier was never completed as planned. Badly damaged by a storm in 1899, it was finally demolished in 1902 after the financial failure of the resort's promoter. Very few traces of the pier survive. Rather more survives of the pier at Westward Ho! constructed in 1870-1. The Pier House restaurant marks the spot (SS 425 292) and the wrought iron stanchions can be seen at low tide. The pier shared a similar history of misfortune as that at Woody Bay, for it was badly damaged by storms within months of opening, then rebuilt in 1873, only to be destroyed by another storm in 1880.

Appledore has Northern Devon's only docks. The first quay had been built around a small creek, a site now occupied by Richmond Dock (SS465 303) and Appledore's present Quay was constructed in the back gardens of houses in Market Street in 1845 and widened to its present extent in 1938-40. Richmond Dock itself was constructed in 1849-56 by William Yeo from Prince Edward Island, Canada and named after Richmond Bay there. Yeo was a classic nineteenth century entrepreneur and built ships in Prince Edward Island to be sailed across the Atlantic and sold to English purchasers who could then have the vessels rigged and fitted out to their requirements in Richmond Dock. Appledore became a centre of ship-building, although the sites, other than Richmond Dock and the modern Bidna covered yard, are now devoid of obvious traces. Bideford too had several shipyards in the nineteenth century. That at Crosspark on the East-the-Water side (SS458 267) disappeared under the railway while Brunswick Wharf (SS457 264) survives a few hundred metres upstream but little suggests its former activity. Other shipbuilding sites were at Bank End (SS456 275) on the site now occupied by the Torridge District Council offices and Cleavehouses (SS456278), just under the Torridge Bridge. Barnstaple had several shipyards including a large yard on the west bank of the Taw just downstream of the Raleigh Cabinet Works (SS556 329). As with Bideford, there is now little visible evidence.

Lighthouses, of which there are six surviving, constitute another distinctive feature of the Northern Devon coastline. The oldest is the Old Light on Lundy (SS132 443), built of local granite in 1819 and some 29 metres tall. However, Lundy Island is often shrouded in fog and the light on the highest point of the island was ineffective and thus the North (SS131 482) and South Lights (SS144 437) , lower on the cliffs, were built to replace it in 1897. On the mainland, lights were constructed at Hartland Point (SS 229278) in 1874, Bull Point (SS 463467) in 1879 and at Foreland Point (SS 754512) in 1900. All are now automated and can be seen from the South West Coastal Path. The entrance to the Taw and Torridge estuaries is now marked by small beacons but a tower light, Barnstaple High Light (SS458 324) once stood at Crow Point and bricks from the keepers' houses may still be found. (JB)

Further reading:

Boyle V and Payne D 1952: *Devon Harbours.* London: Christopher Johnson.

Farr G 1976: *Shipbuilding in North Devon.* Greenwich, National Maritime Museum Maritime Monograph and Report 22.

Railways

Railways almost always make a significant impact on the landscape and thus there is usually a considerable archaeological presence after they have gone. Of all of Northern Devon's railways, only the Bideford, Westward Ho! and Appledore line has left a more subtle legacy. Railway engineers strove to limit gradients to a maximum of 1:40 and so the track bed often required cuttings and embankments which have tended to survive. Railway buildings, in particular stations and goods sheds, have also survived through finding alternative uses, often as private dwellings, although signal boxes have generally been demolished. Exceptions are at Barnstaple Town station and Fremington Quay.

The table below shows the principal dates associated with Northern Devon's railways and it is notable that the first closure, that of the Bideford Westward Ho! and Appledore occurred before the last railway line was opened: the re-gauging of the Torrington to Marland clay line and its extension through to Halwill Junction. Of Northern Devon's approximately 194 kilometres of railway, only 30 kilometres remain open, this being the line from Exeter and Crediton to Barnstaple together with a 1.5 kilometre stretch of the Lynton and Barnstaple Railway reopened from Woody Bay station to Killington Lane. Woody Bay and Barnstaple Junction station buildings are the only ones still in use for railway purposes. Most of the station buildings survive as private residences from Chapelton to Kings Nympton.

Section of railway	Date of opening	Date of closure (passenger traffic)
Fremington-Barnstaple	1848 horse drawn; freight only	1965
Crediton-Barnstaple	1854 (broad gauge)	
Fremington-Bideford	1855 (broad gauge)	1965
Exeter-Crediton-Barnstaple-Bideford	1863 (standard gauge tracks added; through trains from London Waterloo	
Bideford-Torrington	1872	1965
Taunton-South Molton-Barnstaple	1873 (broad gauge)	1966
Barnstaple Junction-Ilfracombe	1874	1970
Exeter-Bideford	1876 broad gauge track removed	1965
Meldon Junction (west of Okehampton)-Holsworthy	1879	1966
Torrington-Marland	1880 (3 foot gauge clay line)	1965
Taunton-Barnstaple	1881 broad gauge converted	1966
Barnstaple Victoria Road-Barnstaple Junction (Barnstaple west curve)	1884	1966
Halwill Junction-Launceston	1886	1966
Holsworthy-Bude	1898	1966
Barnstaple Town-Lynton	1898 (narrow gauge)	1935
Bideford-Westward Ho!	1901	1917
Barnstaple east curve (to allow direct running from Taunton to Ilfracombe)	1905	1966
Westward Ho!-Appledore	1908	1917
Torrington-Halwill Junction	1925	1965

Station buildings and station-master's houses finding other uses than as private houses are the Puffing Billy pub at Torrington (SS479 198) the Pathfield School at the former Barnstaple Town (SS555 332) and a newsagents at Braunton

The preserved signal box at Bideford.

(SS487 365). At Bideford the remaining half of the station buildings has most recently served as offices for Devon County Council. Railway goods sheds have survived less frequently, but good examples are the Grosvenor church at the former Barnstaple Victoria Road (SS567 327), the Museum of British Surfing at Braunton and a conversion to a private dwelling at Bishops Nympton and Molland. Signal boxes were often composite structures with a wooden superstructure above a stone base and examples have survived at Bideford (actually a replica) and Instow, whilst the stone built box at Barnstaple Town has been incorporated into the Pathfield School. At Fremington Quay the signal box is now incorporated in the Heritage Centre attached to the café there. A crossing keeper's house in North Road Bideford (SS448 274) is one of the few substantial structures of the Bideford Westward Ho! and Appledore railway to survive.

The track bed of the Barnstaple-Bideford-Torrington-Marland route and the Barnstaple – Braunton -Ilfracombe route have become parts of the Tarka trail and on them walkers can see over-bridges and under-bridges of stone and wrought iron, as well as various smaller concrete structures such as line side huts and ballast bins made at the Southern Railway's concrete works at Exmouth Junction, Exeter. The eagle-eyed may even notice that the Tarka Trail between Barnstaple and Bideford is slightly wider than between Bideford and Torrington, as the former was originally built to Brunel's broad gauge of seven feet and half an inch (2.135 metres) and the latter built to standard gauge of four feet, eight and a half inches (1.22 metres). The Bideford, Westward Ho! and Appledore line forms part of the South West Coastal Path from Westward Ho! south-west to Cornborough Cliff, but the track bed elsewhere is neither a public right of way nor often easy to discern. The Lynton and Barnstaple railway has Northern Devon's best known piece of railway archaeology in the form of the gently curving viaduct at Chelfham(SS 609 356).

Chelfham Viaduct on the old Barnstaple to Lynton line.

A train arriving at Barnstaple station shortly after the line's inception. (Museum of Barnstaple and North Devon)

There is no access to the viaduct as the parapet has been removed. A stretch of the Holsworthy to Bude line has been opened as a public footpath and cycle way to the west of the town and this takes in the viaduct over the river Deer (SS338 035), notable as an early example of concrete in a major civil engineering structure, although it is built of blocks rather than of moulded reinforced concrete. The track bed of the Barnstaple to Taunton line was used for the A361 North Devon Link road between Barnstaple and South Molton and for the Bray Valley viaduct, the old stone piers of the railway viaduct were re-used and heightened, so that Bremridge tunnel on the railway line was avoided.

Railways often had an impact on the settlement hierarchy and there are good examples in Northern Devon. Halwill Junction was the creation of the railway and it boasted far more facilities than other villages in this remote corner of Northern Devon. Whilst Chulmleigh was on the original route from Barnstaple to

Exeter, it was first by-passed by the new turnpike road and then relegated further by its distance from railway stations at Eggesford and Kings Nympton. Umberleigh benefitted at the expense of Chittlehampton and Atherington, and Bishops Nympton and Molland station (4 kilometers from Bishops Nympton and 3 kilometres from Molland) became the site of autumn stock fairs. (JB)

Further Reading:

Thomas D StJ 1960 (revised edition 1996): *A Regional History of the Railways of Great Britain*: Volume 1 *The West Country,* Newton Abbot: David and Charles.

Mitchell V & Smith K 1995: *Taunton to Barnstaple,* Midhurst: Middleton Press.

Nicholas J & Reeve G 2010: *The North Devon Line: The Southern Railway Route between Exeter and Ilfracombe*, Clophill, Bedforshire: Irwell Press

Resorts

A specialised urban settlement for leisure, the seaside resort, emerged at the turn of the 18th century. In Northern Devon at Ilfracombe this started with the existing small port and at Lynton and Lynmouth with existing village settlements. At Westward Ho! a completely new settlement was created from nothing and a similar process commenced at Woody Bay at the very end of the nineteenth century. Seaside tourism had several origins and Northern Devon's resorts were able to capitalise on them all. Throughout the eighteenth century it had been fashionable to visit spas to drink and bathe in the mineral-rich spring waters. From around 1770, medical men began to extol the virtues of drinking and bathing in sea-water and thus the seaside resort was begun. Because of the wars with France, during the quarter century from 1790, Europe became closed to English grand-tourists and instead the fashionable began to explore their

The late 18th century Bath House at Ilfracombe.

homeland. At about this time also there was a major change in landscape taste with dramatic and sublime scenery replacing the merely picturesque and the coast of Northern Devon offered plenty of this more rugged beauty. The poets Coleridge and Wordsworth visited Lynton in 1797 and Southey visited both Lynton and Ilfracombe in 1799, with J M W Turner making the first of his painting trips in 1811 and so the area became much better known.

The architecture of Northern Devon's resorts reflects changing taste in Georgian and Victorian England. The earliest terraces in Ilfracombe, such as Adelaide and Montpelier Terraces are late-Regency in style and conceal their local stone behind stucco. Ilfracombe's principal bathing beach at this time was the Tunnels and a neo-classical Bath House was constructed for indoor bathing in sea water. Some of the earlier villas for clients to rent for a season were in an 18th century Gothick style, such as Runnymeade House in Ilfracombe, but by the middle of the 19th century the more flamboyant high Victorian Gothic style prevailed. Thus in Westward Ho!, where building did not commence until 1863, the Gothic style is dominant. At Ilfracombe, Westward Ho! and Woody Bay, property companies were behind the early developments and at each a major hotel was among the first building projects. The Ilfracombe Hotel and the Royal Hotel at Westward Ho!, both built in the 1860s have not survived, whilst the Woody Bay Hotel from the mid-1880s was one of the few projects completed by the property company. The Torrs Park estate in Ilfracombe, principally dating from the 1880s contains many splendid high Victorian Gothic villas and the Tors Hotel in Lynmouth(1886) and the Valley of Rocks Hotel in Lynton are other impressive Gothic structures.

The Valley of Rocks Hotel, Lynton

Kingsley Terrace (former Kingsley College), Westward Ho!

All Northern Devon's resorts faced a certain tension between accessibility and exclusivity. The railway made resorts accessible but the gradual democratisation of travel, especially with the granting of holidays with pay, meant that a far wider social mix of visitors became possible. Thus Ilfracombe gradually evolved from a watering place for wealthy titled and retired military personnel to spend a summer season, to a seaside resort catering to middle, lower middle and even skilled working class visitors for their annual week's holiday. Its urban morphology also changed and much of the late 19th century building was of properties to be run as boarding houses. Westward Ho! never achieved complete success as a resort, which was why two terraces within a few years came to be converted into private schools, United Services College (now Kipling Terrace) and Kingsley College (Kingsley Terrace). The late construction of a railway (1902) that did not connect to the rest of the network was in large part responsible. (JB)

Further reading:

Bates J 2005: *Ilfracombe Buildings*. Ilfracombe: Civic Trust.
Bates J 2011: *More Ilfracombe Buildings*. Ilfracombe: Civic Trust.
Cherry B and Pevsner N 1989: *The Buildings of England: Devon*. London: Penguin.

Roads and Route-ways

Roads and other route-ways exist both for short-distance and day-to-day travel, such as from farmsteads to fields, and for more infrequent and longer distance movement between Northern Devon and other parts of the county and the rest of the country. Before the advent of settled agriculture in the Neolithic, when the number of people in England was probably only a few hundred thousand, longer distance movements were more important and this is when the major ridge-way routes were probably established.

The ridgeway route from East Anstey Common via Five Barrows to Wood Barrow, much of which now forms the county boundary still survives as public rights of way and is also associated with barrows. The ridgeway route then runs westwards from Wood Barrow to Blackmoor Gate, again with many barrows but on this section no rights of way now exist. From Blackmoor Gate west to Mullacott Cross the ridgeway again becomes a major public right of way. To some sections of this route the Anglo-Saxon term *herepæþ* ('army road') still attaches in the form of Harepath and possibly Harepie.

Most of Northern Devon's numerous roads and lanes evolved

Converted toll house on the Yeo Vale road near Landcross

with the agricultural landscape and manorial organisation as people moved from farmsteads to fields and gathered at churches for worship and at other centres to attend manorial courts. An essential element of the rural economy was the stock track or drove by which beasts were taken from farmstead to common grazing on the moors and downs. These are recognisable as wide and deeply worn tracks leading onto (often formerly) open land where they may widen out and even fade away. Such tracks leading from the lowland to the highland represent a form of transhumance, that is the movement of stock to summer pastures, as is still seen to day in the mountainous parts of southern Europe. Research by the late landscape historian Harold Fox has demonstrated the existence of transhumance routes around Dartmoor. Had he lived, he might have done the same for Exmoor.

As a cash economy developed, weekly or more infrequent visits to market centres were made and a crude hierarchy of purely parochial and sub-regional routes developed. The Long Bridges over the Taw in Barnstaple and the Torridge in Bideford represented major projects for medieval communities. Both bridges were first constructed in the thirteenth century. At

Bideford, the 24 arches vary considerably in size (from 4 to 8 metres in span) and were first constructed of oak, some of which was exposed during widening work in 1925. The available timber was presumably of differing lengths and simply encased in stone sometime between 1460 and 1480. At Barnstaple the 16 arches are more equal in size ranging from around 6 metres to 7 metres, with most being between 6.5 and 7 metres in span and major rebuilding work in 1910 found no timber and so it is presumed that the bridge was initially built of stone. The three arches closest to the town, the Maiden arches, may possibly have been of wood to allow ships to pass through. These may also have been the arches destroyed by the Royalists in 1645 in their defence of the town.

The 1555 Highways Act gave responsibilities for the maintenance of roads to the relevant parish and most were reluctant to do repairs beyond the absolutely essential. Devon, perhaps more than many other counties, became a place where pack-animals rather than wheeled vehicles prevailed. Pack-horse bridges mark the passage of traders carrying goods to isolated communities and many a narrow, deeply worn footpath probably owes its existence to these men and their ponies. In other parts of the country turnpike trusts were established as early as 1663 to maintain and improve principal roads in return for payments made by travellers. Devon was slow to establish turnpikes and Northern Devon lagged behind the rest of the county. The first trusts were those for Barnstaple (1763) and Bideford (1764), with others established in the later eighteenth and nineteenth century, with the very last being that for Combe Martin to Ilfracombe in 1866. The trusts first took in hand existing roads, often ridgeway routes and only in the early nineteenth century did they embark on a major programme of road building to give easier gradients and sweeping curves and tending to follow river valleys. Thus the Taw Valley route from Barnstaple south-eastwards to Exeter replaced the older ridgeway route after 1828 and by-passed Chulmleigh. Other roads from this period include

A Barnstaple Turnpike milestone at Gammaton Cross.

the Barnstaple Trust's valley route to Ilfracombe via Muddiford, the Bideford Trust's Yeo Vale road from Landcross to Bradworthy and the Torrington Trust's route via Beaford to Winkleigh. Characteristic features of these routes are the toll-houses, which were usually situated so that they commanded both the new road and older routes. Almost the last act of the Barnstaple Trust was to erect 105 granite milestones along its routes in 1879. Most of these still survive. The turnpike trusts were progressively wound up in the period 1870-1890, with responsibilities for highway maintenance being transferred to Devon County Council and the County assumed responsibility for all roads under the 1894 Local Government Act. At the final dissolution of Northern Devon's turnpike trusts, they had responsibility for nearly 300 miles (c 480 kilometres) of road. (JB)

Further Reading

Lowe M C 1990: The Turnpike Trusts in Devon and their roads, 1753-1889, *Transactions of the Devonshire Association* 122, 47-69.

Rogers W H 1942: Barnstaple Turnpike Trust, *Transactions of the Devonshire Association* 74, 139-168

Whiting F D 1948: Bideford Bridge, *Transactions of the Devonshire Association* 80, 127-136

Romans (AD43-410)

Despite recent finds indicating Romano-British industrial activity on the western edge of Exmoor, Romans remain elusive in the north of Devon. In fact it has long been thought that Devon and Cornwall as a whole were largely ignored by the Romans and that 'the Romans never came to North Devon'. It is difficult to believe that any part of Britain under Roman control for almost 400 years was 'off limits'. The Southwest, like all other parts of the country would have been valued for its resources and the fact that Roman coins are found throughout Devon must mean that the region had some sort of economic

relationship with the Roman world. Recent major finds at Ipplepen, south-west of Newton Abbot suggest the need for a reassessment of the Roman period in this part of England.

Fragments of Roman Pottery from Brayford, displaying a variety of wares. Numerous comma-shaped pieces of pot rim like that in the centre were found. These seem to have been used as 'feet' on which to stand a vessel.

There is no doubt that during the invasion phase of the occupation, the Roman army, specifically the Second Augustan Legion, penetrated far into the south-west of England. It has long been known that at Martinhoe (SS663 493) and at Old Burrow (SS788 493) on the Exmoor coast near County Gate there are earthworks that are interpreted as Roman military signal stations. Old Burrow is well preserved, while the Martinhoe site has been badly damaged by ploughing, though still recognisable. Both are readily accessible from the Coast Path. Dated to the mid- to later first century AD, these establishments probably kept watch for a short period over the activities of the Silures in the Bristol Channel. Another short-lived military feature of Northern Devon is a possible marching camp identified by aerial photography near Alverdiscott. Together with forts at Tiverton, North Tawton and Okehampton and of course the legionary fortress at Exeter, these represent the first century military phase of the Roman occupation. It is tempting to think that there might have been a Roman naval base somewhere in the Taw-Torridge estuary, but there is as yet no evidence of this.

Roman brooch-pin and coins from the Barnstaple area.

At the end of the first century the Second Augustan Legion left Exeter and the military occupation of the South-West came to an end.

Whereas elsewhere in Britain Roman forts were garrisoned right up until the early 5th century and civil society developed within a context of military-civil administration, the Southwest appears to have been left to its own devices. However, being geographically a part of the Roman province of Britannia, the Southwest was a recipient of Roman goods and its inhabitants would have needed officially minted coinage in order to pay their unavoidable taxes. In addition, the region would have contributed to the economy in the form of livestock and mineral resources.

Strong evidence of the latter has come out of excavations during the last decade at and near Brayford. Throughout the village of Brayford there is widespread evidence of the smelting of iron ore brought down from Exmoor in the Roman period. At a site known as Tanglebray Barn South West Archaeology excavated in 2002 a number of working terraces with evidence of smelting and smithing together with over 1300 sherds of Roman pottery including southwestern grey wares, black-burnished ware (from Dorset), Samian ware (from Gaul) and amphorae (from Spain). It is evident both from here, from elsewhere in Brayford and not too far away at Sherracombe Ford that the working of Exmoor iron extended from the pre-Roman Iron Age well into the Roman period when the ultimate market for the product would have been the Roman army. Again it is tempting to speculate on the possible use of the Taw-Torridge estuary, since transporting the product downhill to the estuary and then by water would have been easier than carting it eastwards over land. The seaborne destination might have been Abonae (Avonmouth) or Venta Silurum (Caerwent).

As for artefacts, there are a few recorded finds of Roman pottery while Roman coins have turned up occasionally over the years and are widely found by metal detectorists, some of them in (so far) small hoards. The dates range right up to the time of Theodosius in the late 4th century. The presence of coins must mean that the indigenous people of Devon were fully drawn into the Roman economy, though the extent of their romanisation is open to research. Finds of Roman 'brooches' (fibulae) around Fremington and around Tawstock suggest some influence on dress and are a further indication of trade between a partially romanised Southwest and the core of Roman Britain.

By the time the Roman administration of Britain collapsed in the early 5th century, Devon and Cornwall had been part of the Roman world for around 400 years. In AD 212 the Emperor Caracalla had decreed that all free men within the Empire should be treated as Roman citizens enjoying all the rights and obligations that went with this status. Thus, when the soldiers and officials drifted away, the indigenous people of Britain continued to regard themselves as Romans retaining continental links, continuing to trade with the Mediterranean, while the use of Latin endured side by side with traditional Brittonic speech. Echoes of this linguistic heritage lingered probably into the 6th or 7th century when, between Parracombe and Lynton, a memorial stone was erected to the memory of Cavudus –who bore a Brittonic name – son of Civilis, whose name was thoroughly Roman.

So, after the first century military phase of Roman occupation, it is probably true that few actual Romans came to North Devon, it being perhaps too remote and difficult of access. However, it is probably also true that the people of the area became at least partially romanised and were economically and culturally involved in the Roman world, the influence of which lingered well after the rest of Roman Britain had become Saxon England. (TG)

Further Reading:

Pearce S 1981: *The Archaeology of South West Britain*, London.
Todd M 1987: *The South-West to AD 1000*, London.

Rural Settlement:

We should begin with one or two clarifications. To avoid ambiguity, geographers and landscape historians use the term 'settlement' to comprise hamlets, villages and small towns, in fact anywhere where human communities have set up a permanent home. Among settlements a distinction is then made between nucleated and dispersed settlements. A typical nucleated settlement might be represented by the sort of community you see in a TV programme such as 'Midsomer Murders', for most people a 'typical' English village with its church, manor house, vicarage, pub and cottages around the village green. In fact this kind of settlement is more typical of the Midland and eastern counties than of the Southwest. Devon is principally characterised by 'dispersed settlement' represented by hamlets of two or three farms scattered about a parish, the centre of which may boast no more than the church, a barton farm or small cluster of farms, perhaps a manor house and a few cottages – East Down, for example, near Combe Martin. With the addition of cottages and a few grander houses, some hamlets may have

Molland, a typical Northern Devon settlement with church, manor house and farms.

grown over time into an irregular cluster of dwellings around the parish church, as, for example, at Westleigh, near Bideford. However, there exist also in the Devonshire landscape a number of 'over large' villages which do not fall readily into either classification. The origins of this settlement pattern are the subject of ongoing research, because it is by no means clear how it came about. Finally it is important to understand that rural settlement can be quite dynamic with settlements growing or contracting, moving across the landscape and in some cases disappearing.

The typical prehistoric settlement of this region is probably represented by the hillslope enclosure (see 'Enclosures') or 'round', an ovoid or sub-rectangular banked and ditched enclosure containing a couple of round-houses, animal pens and workshops and accompanied by a system of small, irregular fields. The remains of this type of settlement are scattered across the county. At some time in the post-Roman period, probably in the 7th-8th century, the ancient pattern of enclosed settlements gave way to open settlements or hamlets with enclosed, intensively cultivated field-systems. In other parts of England, principally in a swathe running from Dorset north-eastwards to Yorkshire, the Middle Saxon period (7th-9th century) saw a re-organisation of settlements – probably from dispersed hamlets - into nucleated villages with extensive open-field systems. With one or two exceptions, this movement did not affect West Somerset, Devon and Cornwall. Instead the region developed a system of 'convertible husbandry', in which small farming communities tended an intensively cultivated infield with an occasionally cultivated outfield, while grazing cattle, sheep, pigs and goats on the extensive uplands. Within the infield – possibly known as a *worðig*- the land was subdivided into strips, the responsibility for which was dispersed among the tenants. Remnants of this system were still to be seen in the early 19th century, for example at South Radworthy (North Molton), Hele (Parracombe) and Parkham Ash.

It seems clear that this system of farm hamlets did not exist in a vacuum, but that there were centres from which power emanated and which held together scattered settlements in a network of obligations and tribute. To landscape archaeologists and historians these centres are known as 'capita' (Latin for 'heads'). Such territorial units are often called 'multiple or federal estates' and were distinguished in Anglo-Saxon nomenclature as a tūn ('ton'). By the time of the Domesday survey in the 1080s the manorial system had developed with power descending from the King through a hierarchy of supporters and dependents. The 'capita' had become head manors held directly by the King. In the North Devon area Braunton, South Molton, Tawstock, Witheridge and Hartland were among the King's manors. Barnstaple was a borough held by the King. Numbers of these had probably been 'capita' for many centuries, quite possibly since before Devon became part of Wessex in the 7th/8th century. Among them also however, were manors which had begun life as minor settlements, but had become elevated.

Tawstock, Langtree and Littleham were probably such elevated settlements and probably also Barnstaple itself which may have originated as a minor settlement, a riverside trading post perhaps, within a territory whose 'caput' may have been Braunton or (Bishops) Tawton or even Pilton.

The process of settlement elevation went on in a rather different manner after the Conquest. In the 13th and 14th centuries there was a movement among manorial lords to transform their holdings of scattered hamlets into 'boroughs'. Already before the Conquest Barnstaple was a borough inhabited by burgesses who were essentially free of the tenurial obligations of service that villeins owed to their lord. In return the burgesses paid an agreed rent for a house and a plot of land (a 'burgage plot') within a borough, the lay-out of which was prescribed by the lord of the manor and which generally followed a common pattern (see 'Towns'). A number of boroughs maintained their status into modern times and went on to become small towns, but others failed – Rackenford and Sheepwash, for example - and are seen today as villages, some of them 'over large' such as Hartland or Combe Martin.

The history of rural settlement over the last thousand to fifteen hundred years has been a history of change. Some originally obscure settlements have risen in status and expanded and/or become manorial and parish centres, while others have declined and in some cases disappeared. A prime example of an abandoned settlement is Badgeworthy (SS793 445), remotely located on Exmoor, where the remains of its cottages can still be seen amid the bracken. Others have drifted across country, so that what we see now as the 'village' is distant from its medieval ancestor. Challacombe on the road to Simonsbath now lies a kilometre to the east of Barton Town, its ancestral centre, Instow has likewise moved away from its church and barton, Parracombe and Clawton now lie in valley bottoms below their ancient 'Town' on the high ground. In fact wherever we see 'Town Farm' or 'Barton Town' or some such we should assume

Barton Town, Challacombe with 'humps and bumps' of the reduced original settlement in the field beside the churchyard.

that this is the medieval centre of the community from which settlement has possibly strayed.

Finally, it is important to remember that climate and topograhy have determined that the rural economy of Devon has traditionally been characterised by both 'horn' and 'corn'. While practically all settlements had their arable fields, they also had herds of cattle and flocks of sheep as well as pigs and goats. In the summer, when grain crops had to be tended, it was important to provide grazing for the animals. Studies have shown that the practice of transhumance was widespread: animals were taken in spring from the lowland to the upland, onto the downs and moors and also onto coastal marshes and into woodland, returning to the home settlement in the autumn. During the summer they had to be tended, quite possibly by young women and youths, who would probably create temporary shelters close to their charges. In time, as population expanded and pressure on land grew, a number of such seasonal settlements would have become permanent settlements. The whole question of transhumance and the transformation of seasonal into permanent settlements has been closely studied by the landscape historian, the late Harold Fox and his work 'Dartmoor's Alluring Uplands' (2012) is well worth consulting. (TG)

Further Reading:

Aston M 1985: *Interpreting the Landscape: Landscape Archaeology and History,* London: Routlege.
Fox H 2012: *Dartmoor's Alluring Uplands*, Exeter University Press.
Turner S 2006: *Medieval Devon and Cornwall: Shaping an Ancient Countryside*, Macclesfield: Windgather Press.

Stones:

That is, 'standing stones', ie. stones standing in the landscape from prehistory as opposed to those possibly set up by farmers as scratching-posts for their livestock. This is a distinction which it may be difficult to make, since a stone standing in pasture and obviously used by animals to relieve itches may be prehistoric anyway. A small cluster of examples exists within grid square SS47-46 between Ilfracombe and Mortehoe, at least one of which is readily visible from a footpath. However, there are some standing stones in the farmed landscape which, from their impressive size, are probably prehistoric. Good examples are to be seen on Kentisbury Down at SS639 440 and on Mattocks Down at SS600 439. A readily accessible standing stone is the Pilton Longstone on the roadside at SS554 343. Now rare and scattered, it is probable that in the past there were many more standing stones now cleared away or broken up by farmers. The random nature of their preservation makes it impossible to discern any purpose, so that we have no clear way of understanding them, though some people have guessed that they may have helped prehistoric people to find their way across the land.

More likely to be ritualistic in their purpose are the stone circles, stone rows and other stone settings which survive best on the high ground of Exmoor, although there is also the elusive stone row beside the Taw estuary at Yelland (SS490 330). In fact apart from the very visible and impressive Longstone on Challacombe Common, most of Exmoor's stone settings are

The Longstone on Challacombe Common with Wood Barrow on the skyline

elusive or at least hard to find because they are small, so that the ironic term 'miniliths' has been coined to distinguish them from megaliths.

The stone monuments found throughout the British Isles are thought to date from the Neolithic to early Bronze Age periods, and this is probably true also of the Exmoor and North Devon examples. Within the area of interest that we have defined in this A-Z there are no surviving stone circles, although a report from the 18th century suggests that there may have been one on Mattocks Down (see below). On West Exmoor however, there are a number of known stone rows and stone settings, the latter represented by geometrically placed groups of stones and apparently unique to Exmoor. Well publicised, but again elusive, is the 'White Ladder' stone row on Five Barrows Hill (SS73-37). When shrinkage of the peat in a dry summer makes the row traceable, it is seen to be over 400m in length and to consist of closely spaced blocks of white quartz. Another long stone row is on Cheriton Ridge near to the head of Farley Water. In fact this area (centred at, say, SS75-44) is particularly rich in stone monuments, while the upper reaches of Badgeworthy Water too (centred at, say, SS79-44) are well populated with stone settings. Among the geometrical stone settings of Exmoor are four 'quincunxes' consisting of five stones set like the five pips on a playing card. The purpose of such an arrangement remains completely obscure.

Although the emphasis here is on the uncultivated land of high Exmoor, some indication of what may have been lost at lower altitudes is gained from the following 18th century account of stones on Mattocks Down, where now only one stone remains, and that recently shattered by a lightning strike:

On Maddoc-common, one stone is of a remarkable size, and one only. It is of a conic figure, not so large at the base, as near its center, occasioned by the sheep rubbing against it. At the center, it measures fifteen feet four inches. The height, about which I could not be so exact, I take to be eleven feet, if not more. In a line parallel to this great stone, from south to north, and at the distance of twenty-four paces, lies a trunk of stone, about a foot from the ground, whose diameter is two feet eight inches. About twelve paces distant from this, in a line from west to east, is a stone not a foot above the ground, and about a foot in diameter. Were there another to correspond to the large one, these four would include a space of ground, whose opposite sides would be equal.

I counted more than an hundred clusters of stone in different parts. In some places, six, eight, or more are to be seen together, but not remarkable for their height. At one groupe of six, the eye is particularly engaged. These stand circular-wise, and are the only ones in which the circular figure can be discovered. At the distance of four paces from this circle, is the trunk of a stone, nearly three feet above the surface, whose diameter measures about three feet. (Respondent to Dean Milles Questionnaire)

It is clear from this description that what was once complex is now reduced to very little and with that reduction has gone the possibility of understanding such stone arrangements. Mattocks Down is unlikely to have been unique and it is quite probable that across Northern Devon, farming activity has removed other such complex stone formations, so that we are left today with the impression that stone settings are exclusive to the high moors. One thing that we definitely lack and appear to have lost is the 'dolmen' or 'quoit' type monument, of which there are numbers of examples in Cornwall. This is the stone formation in which a large, flat stone lies on top of stone uprights and represents the denuded remains of a probably Neolithic chambered tomb. The former presence of these may be indicated by the quite widespread place-name Shilstone from Old English *scylf-st n* ('shelf-stone'). (TG)

See also the entry on Inscribed Stones.

Further Reading:

Grinsell L V 1970: *The Archaeology of Exmoor: Bideford Bay to Bridgwater*, Newton Abbot.

Riley H and Wilson-North R 2001: *The Field Archaeology of Exmoor*, English Heritage.

Submerged forests and environmental change

In many places around the coast of England and Wales, there are submerged forests. That at Westward Ho! (SS430 292) has been known for nearly two centuries but is only visible after winter storms have scoured the beach sand that usually covers the site. Up to 70 trunks have been found and some measure roughly 45 centimetres in diameter. Those that have been identified to species are oaks. The surface into which they are rooted has been radio-carbon dated to approximately 6,300 years BP. This surface also contains a kitchen midden, with remains of roe and red deer, aurochs, fish and mussel shells. At that time sea-level was some 7 metres lower than at present and the shoreline would have been several hundred metres further out to sea.

About 10,800 BP, sea level was some 40 metres lower than today and Lundy Island was still attached to the mainland, although shortly to be isolated by rising sea-level. In a further two thousand years, the Straits of Dover would be formed and England separated from the European mainland. Sea levels continued to rise in the succeeding millennia but even some 2,000 years BP, sea-level was 4 metres lower than today and the Bronze Age stone row at Yelland (SS492 328) which now is barely visible through the mud would have stood well clear of the high-water mark.

Other evidence of environmental change comes from pollen recovered from organic deposits and radio-carbon dates from wood and charcoal in such deposits. The picture that emerges from samples taken by auger on the flanks of Exmoor is one of peat starting to accumulate from around 7,400 BP in slightly moister conditions than prevail today. Considerable evidence of the loss of forest cover is provided by the sudden fall in the abundance of tree pollen from around 6,700 BP and this almost certainly occurred as a result of human activity. Samples of preserved pollen indicate a continued decline of tree cover through the Neolithic and Bronze Age periods while pollen from grasses and cereals (which are almost impossible to distinguish) and from weeds of cultivation increase in abundance. It is generally thought that by the Romano-British period, Northern Devon had not a great deal more woodland than it has today

Raised pebble beach at Westward Ho! (Paul Madgett)

Evidence of longer term climatic and environmental change comes from the famous Barnstaple elephants. Tusks and teeth were discovered in the Summerland Street area of Barnstaple in 1844. Subsequent analysis has shown these to have come from the straight-tusked elephant (*Palaeoloxodon antiquus*) and may well date from around 120,000 BP. Unfortunately nineteenth century antiquaries were very casual about the contexts from which their finds came and so precise dating is now impossible. At this time, known as the Ipswichian inter-glacial, climate was several degrees warmer than today and sea-levels could well have been 10 metres higher. This probably would have made the Summerland Street area an intertidal swamp, high tides extending much further up the Taw and Torridge than at present.

At Saunton (SS 445 377 and westwards) and at Croyde (from Baggy Point to Down End), also at Westward Ho! (SS423 292), there are ancient beach deposits in the low cliffs probably dating to these Ipswichian interglacial times, extending to well above present high-tide level. These deposits are referred to as 'raised beaches'. At that time our present Taw-Torridge estuary would have had a much wider mouth, Barnstaple/Bideford Bay extending east of Fremington Quay, with no Braunton or Northam Burrows.

Some giant boulders, derived from as far away as NW Scotland, occur along these Saunton and Croyde shores. Known as "erratics", they were probably emplaced by glacial ice, from a period pre-dating the Ipswichian interglacial, the famous Saunton Red Granite (SS440 379) being sealed in by the raised beach deposits at the base of the cliff. Possibly the Northern Devon coastal fringe was over-run by the southern edge of a huge ice-sheet at this time, a few erratic boulders having been found on top of Baggy Point at Croyde. A lobe of this early ice-sheet reached up what is now the Taw estuary, depositing the boulder clay at Fremington. Geologists are undecided exactly when this occurred, as each glacial episode tends to obliterate evidence of those occurring before.

The Raised Beach deposits are overlain by frost-shattered debris derived from the slopes above, termed 'head' (being at the 'head' of the cliffs). This material records an increasingly colder climate, starting perhaps 10,000 years after the elephants occupied southern England, sea-level receding till it was over 100 metres lower than today. During the ice advance known as

The cliff below Saunton Down. At the foot of the cliff and above the modern beach the raised beach is seen as naturally cemented sand known as sand-rock.

the Devensian Northern Devon would have been subjected to permafrost and tundra like conditions, frost-shattering giving rise to those Head deposits. This glacial period was to last, with several slightly warmer episodes, for virtually 100,000 years.

In Northern Devon there is at present no evidence for human occupation in these earlier periods, but Kent's Cavern and other sites in the south of the county have shown that early humans did live in Devon for parts of this very lengthy epoch. (PM and JB)

Further reading:
Campbell S et al (eds.) 1998: Geological Conservation Review Series: *Quaternary of South-West England* London.
Durrance E M and Laming D J C (eds) 1982: *The Geology of Devon*. Exeter.
Keene P (1996) *Classic Landforms of the North Devon Coast.* Sheffield:
Preece C (2008) *A Field Guide to the Archaeology of the Taw and Torridge Estuaries*, Bideford.

The Tithe Survey

An invaluable resource for reconstructing the rural landscape early in the 19th century is the Tithe Survey. Dating from medieval times, a tithe was a tenth part of all produce which all parishioners were bound to render to the Church. By the early 19th century the traditional system had become so unwieldy that change was due, hence in 1836 the Commutation of the Tithe Act was passed, preparing the way for the tithe in kind to be replaced by annual money payments for the support of the parish church, its clergy and any other persons holding a right to the tithe. To this end, all parishes where the tithe still existed (and this in practice meant virtually all of Devon's parishes) were to be surveyed, with land-ownership, occupation and land-use for all parcels of land and their size recorded. In many instances,

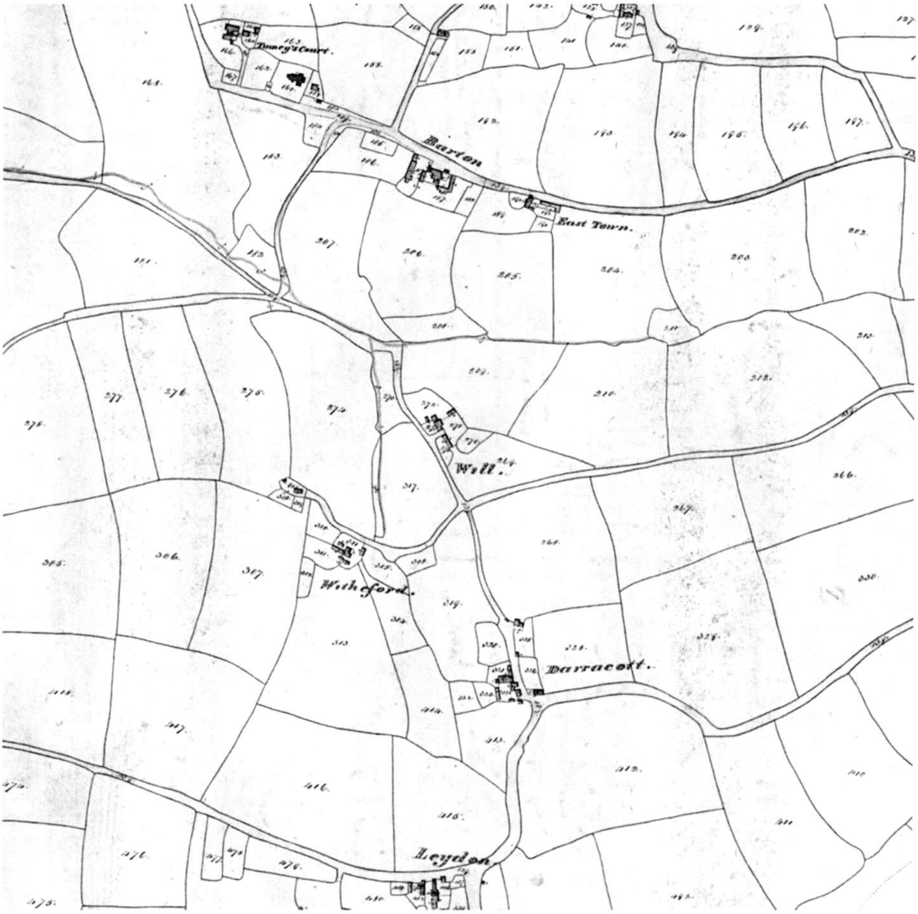

A section of the Welcombe tithe map

local meetings accepted the suggested money replacements, but in other cases, a formal award was made by the Tithe Commissioners in London.

The Tithe Surveys took place usually between 1837 and 1842 and the actual survey comprised a large scale plan, the Tithe Map, usually at a scale of 1inch to 3 chains with each parcel identified by a reference number, together with the Apportionment, a tabulation of all parcels, usually in alphabetical order of land-owner. For each parcel of land, the owner, the occupier, its name, land-use, area and valuation are given. The Act and the Chief

Commissioner of Tithes had specified the land use categories to be used. However, it is clear that the local men who acted as surveyors and valuers on the ground adopted their own interpretations of the official categories (some surveyors in Northern Devon seemed reluctant to classify any grassland as meadow, for instance) and some also made further sub-divisions and distinctions. Thus for pasture, some surveyors offered the qualifications of coarse, furzy, marshy, moory and rough.

The value to the landscape historian and archaeologist is that, apart from individual manor surveys, the Tithe Survey is the first fairly comprehensive large scale mapping and land-use inventory available and is comparable nationally to the Domesday survey of 1086. Some scholars feel that it is possible to use the Tithe Survey to reconstruct late medieval estates and former open fields. Others would be more cautious. What the Tithe Survey does show is Victorian agriculture before the Repeal of the Corn Laws opened the country to cheap grain imports, and the railway network made possible regional specialisation within British agriculture. The Table below shows the broad patterns of land-use in the Tithe Survey across 41 parishes in Northern Devon. It needs to be stressed that the large amount of arable land is a measure of the land actively tilled in some form of a rotation and that perhaps in any one year only a third or so of this would be under cereals. The similarity to the land-use distribution at Domesday is striking.

Percentage of land in various forms of use c 1840
for a sample of 41 northern Devon parishes

Land use	Percentage of total area
Arable	53.5
Meadow	5.2
Pasture	31.5
Gardens and orchards	1.6
Farm buildings and waste	1.1
Woodland	7.1

The Devon tithe maps are available for inspection in the Devon Record Office, Great Moor House, Exeter. They have been digitised and should eventually be accessible on line, as in fact the apportionments already are. (JB)

Further reading:
Kain R J P & Prince C (1985) *The Tithe Surveys of England and Wales.* Cambridge:Cambridge University Press.

Towns

The term 'town' is a rather broad one. Avoiding, therefore, the niceties of definition, this entry will deal mainly with the larger towns of Barnstaple, Bideford and Ilfracombe and will touch on South Molton, Holsworthy, Great Torrington, Hatherleigh and Northam all of which have a town council. Historically the essential prerequisites for the evolution from rural settlement to town were the acquisition of a borough charter and a market charter, for both of which application had to be made to the King. The high point of borough creation was the 13th century, during which period some 30 boroughs were created in Devon either by ecclesiastical or secular lords. These were followed in the 14th century by a further 21, making Devon the county with the largest number of medieval boroughs. Relatively few of these have survived as 'towns', but a search through historic records may reveal the former borough status of what is now a large village – Chulmleigh is a case in point, as is Hartland. Somewhat more accessible however, is the physical evidence. Typically a new borough was laid out to a plan. There was a main street on either side of which were long, narrow burgage plots lying perpendicular to the street and each held in free tenure. The street might widen out at one end to form a market place, often now no longer recognisable having been filled in in the post-medieval centuries. Located to one side would often be the church and perhaps the manor house. This basic plan is frequently obscured by later developments, but can perhaps be recognised on a large scale 19th century Ordnance Survey maps. Pilton (created 1205 by the Abbot of Malmesbury), Winkleigh (created 1237) and Sheepwash (created 1230) are examples. This is not the place to go into the reasons for the creation of boroughs; suffice it to say that it was principally economic.

Among the towns of northern Devon, only Barnstaple is attested as having been a borough before 1066, when it was one of the four boroughs of Devon. In the guise of 'Pilton' it is listed in the Burghal Hidage, an Anglo-Saxon document listing the defended 'burhs' established as a defence against the Danes. Domesday Book records (1086) that the borough of Barnstaple had 40 burgesses within the borough and 9 without. Since 1066 23 houses had been destroyed (possibly occasioned by the building of the castle), so the borough must have already been well developed and probably lay within the area defined by the rivers Taw and Yeo and what is now Boutport Street, or quite

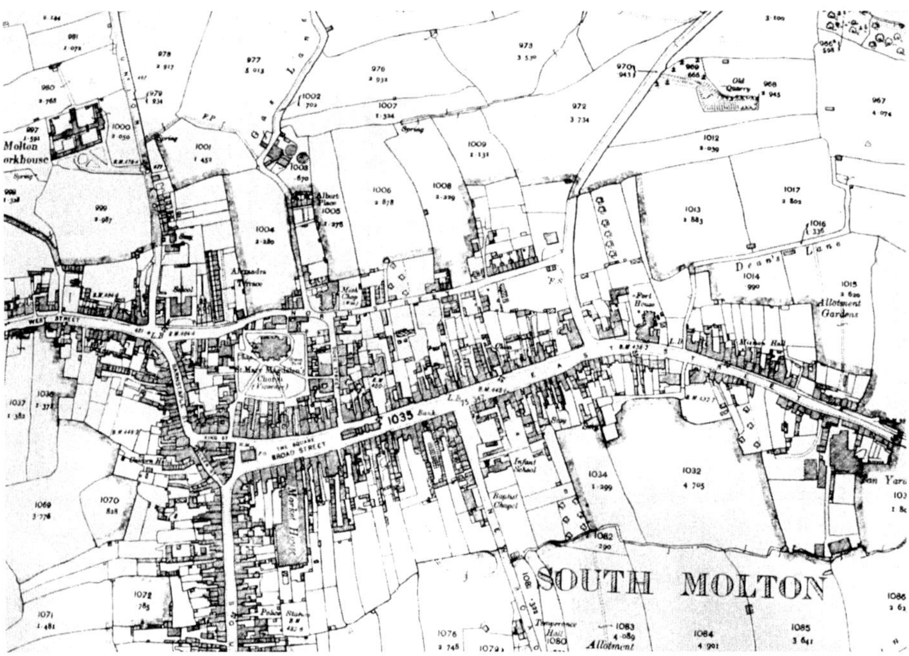

The early 20th century map of South Molton clearly illustrates the lay-out of a medieval borough with main street, long burgage plots on either side and a market place at one end. South Molton received its borough charter around AD 1200.

An early19th century view of a part of the Barnstaple Strand. In the centre is the Watergate at the bottom of Cross Street and beside it is the Quay Hall, formerly St Nicholas' Chapel. To the right of the Quay Hall is the fish market and visible behind it the Star Inn. All of these features were swept away in 19th century efforts at improvement. (Museum of Barnstaple and North Devon)

possibly Green Lane, and may already have been enclosed within earth banks or walls. Still today the lay-out of the town centre shows signs of having been built to a plan with at its core a main street and long individual plots lying perpendicular to it on either side. It has been claimed that Barnstaple is the oldest borough in England dating from AD 930, the time of King Athelstan; unfortunately this claim is based on a charter of doubtful authenticity. It is clear however, that by the 10th century Barnstaple was regionally important since it had a mint, whose coins have been found as far away as Dublin and Scandinavia.

For such an ancient town, Barnstaple today displays rather little of its medieval origins. By Leland's day (early 16th century) the town walls were 'almost clean fallen', though the gates remained until the 19th century. The castle, probably first built in the 11th century, was a ruin by the mid-14th century, nothing remaining today but the prominent castle mound (motte) beside Castle Green. Excavations on Castle Green in the 1970s revealed that the motte and the inner bailey partly overlay a pre-Conquest Saxon cemetery with at least 150 graves. Barnstaple Bridge (the Long Bridge) was first erected near the lowest fording point of the Taw in the late 13th century. Standing at its eastern end was a chantry chapel dedicated to St Thomas-a-Becket. Other chapels were St Nicholas' Chapel attached to the Water Gate at the lower end of Cross Street, All Hallows by the North Gate and – the only now surviving – St Anne's Chapel by the parish church. The parish church of St Mary was dedicated or rededicated in 1318, but certainly has earlier origins. Now completely forgotten except for certain street names is the Cluniac Priory of St Mary Magadelene built outside the walls on the north side of the borough and endowed by Judhel of Totnes in about 1107.

From the post-medieval centuries we have built features which mirror the prosperity of Barnstaple derived from the Atlantic trade. Most prominent among these is Queen Anne's Walk, a colonnaded building beside the town quay and housing the 'tome stone' on which merchants struck their bargains. Elaborate 17th century plaster ceilings are to be seen in some buildings, most strikingly in the restaurant known as The Bank next door to the Royal and Fortescue Hotel; this was originally a prosperous merchant's house. Somewhat tucked away are the Horwood's almshouses in Church Lane, dating from the mid-17th century, together with the Poor Maids' School of similar date and in the same lane. In Litchdon Street are the Penrose Almshouses , established in 1627 by John Penrose, merchant and exporter. Next door to the Penrose Almshouses was, until recently, the Exeter Inn the roof timbers of which have been dated by dendrochronology to about 1600. Litchdon Street was for centuries the main route leading out of the town across tidal marshland, and the Exeter Inn may have been the last or first hostelry encountered by travellers.

Spells of prosperity and a spirit of urban improvement from the late 18th into the 20th century have served to obscure much of the earlier historic character of Barnstaple's buildings, so that a walk along the town's main streets reveals a variety of 19th century façades, some of their features quite whimsical if you

Barnstaple Square: On the left, the Museum, formerly the North Devon Athenaeum, 1872, centre, Bridge Chambers 1874, right, Bridge Buildings 1844. The Square originated in 1723 when the land was reclaimed from tidal marsh.

look up, and later 20th century commercial blandness. The one building in the High Street which, with its half-timbered façade, appears to retain any historic character is the former Three Tuns Inn, now Pizza Express; unfortunately this appearance is pure pastiche, the work of local architect and antiquarian Bruce Oliver and dates from 1946. Inside however, there is much of interest. The North Country Inn in Mermaid Walk (now converted to a restaurant) is also worth a visit, retaining a number of early features. The Guild Hall, as it now appears, was designed by Thomas Lee in 1826 to replace an earlier building which stood at the High Street end of Paternoster Row. Butchers' Row, built on the site of the earlier Butchers' Market and completed in 1855, represents a nationally rare instance of a street dedicated to a single trade. Built at the same time, the Pannier Market , designed by R.D.Gould, replaced an earlier 18th century Market House in the High Street. These are just a few of the prominent features of the town. There are many others which repay close investigation.

Until recent times Barnstaple and Bideford had a thriving and important pottery industry. The earliest evidence of pottery production in Barnstaple comes from a late 13th century kiln

Number 28 Bridgeland Street, Bideford, the best preserved of the late 17th century merchants' houses

excavated in the area of the library. This same area has provided substantial evidence of a pottery industry active well into the 18th century. The name of Cross Street, a corruption of Crock Street, suggests that this area too had a community of potters, though at what period we do not know. A gap in the chronology of Barnstaple pottery production has recently been made good by excavations at the rear of the former Exeter Inn in Litchdon Street, where abundant evidence of 15th and 16th century activity has come to light. Products of the many kilns in both Barnstaple and Bideford as well as Great Torrington found their way as far away as Newfoundland and New England in the USA and even Australia and the Caribbean.

Barnstaple's rival, Bideford was, for a period of about 50 years in the late 17th/early 18th century the premier town of North Devon, its prosperity largely resting on the tobacco trade with Virginia and on the Newfoundland fishery. In its earlier life however, it did not have the status of Barnstaple. Nevertheless, in 1086 (Domesday Book) Bideford was a valuable manor held by Queen Matilda, having considerable areas of ploughland, pasture and woodland together with a fishery and rendering £16 in tax. Under William Rufus the manor was given to the Grenvilles who, in 1217, made it into a borough and later in the same century obtained a charter for a market and a fair. At about the same period Bideford bridge was built, initially in oak timber, but later clad in stone, the unequal timbers dictating the varied dimensions of the bridge arches. Along the Torridge ship-building developed and a new quay was begun in 1663. By the late 17th century Bideford rivalled Topsham and London in number of vessels plying the Newfoundland fisheries.

Testimony to the wealth of Bideford's merchants at that time is what has been described as an early – perhaps the earliest - instance of town-planning in the municipal sense. Feoffees of the Bideford Bridge Trust, looking to suitably accommodate and profit from the newly wealthy, conceived a plan to build a new street in the northern part of the borough and in 1690 Nathaniel Gascoyne was commissioned to produce a design. The street was to be 40 feet wide, the houses of two storeys, the whole to be finished within two years. An application by the Feoffees for letters patent dated 4th May 1699 (NDRO: BBT add1/92) records in detail the 'great and glorious work' that had been completed and was now Bridgeland Street. When Daniel Defoe passed through Bideford in 1724 he remarked on 'a new and spacious street … broad as the High Street of Exeter, well built, and … well inhabited with considerable and wealthy merchants, who trade to most parts of the world.' Despite more recent developments, the patrician character of Bridgeland Street can still be appreciated, especially at Number 28.

Unlike Barnstaple, whose lay-out suggests deliberate design from the very beginning, Bideford seems to have grown up in a more piecemeal, ad hoc fashion. Compared with other medieval boroughs in Devon, the lay-out and street pattern of Bideford is

Bideford Town Hall and Library 1905 and Bridge Buildings 1882.

unusual. Most frequently we can recognise at the heart of such settlements a lay-out conforming to the pattern described above. In Bideford there is a High Street with what appear to be burgage plots on both sides, the church nearby and even the site of the former manor house adjacent. However, the existing market place is set apart, lying to the south of the High Street at the head of Bridge Street. The burgage plots on the south side of the High Street appear to extend to the market place, the buildings on the north side of the market place occupying their southern ends. It is suggested that Bideford may originally have had a market in the usual High Street location, but that at a later period the market was transposed away from the High Street to its present site. Buildings around the market show signs of a 17th/18th century origin, while the present Pannier Market was built over the market-place in the 19th century.

The late-developer among the trio of larger towns is Ilfracombe, whose growth was stimulated by the development of a fashion for sea bathing in the late 18th century. Offering a rare sheltered harbour on the rocky North Devon coast, it seems that it was of value to Iron Age people who constructed a promontory fort on Hillsborough overlooking the harbour. By 1086 (Domesday Book) the Saxon manor known as 'Alfred's combe' (nothing to do with King Alfred) had become modestly useful to the Exchequer with a taxable value of £4. By the mid-13th century, when it was held by the Champernoune family, the manor had been turned into a borough and in 1326 there were 49 burgages along the High Street. The characteristic borough lay-out is visible on the tithe map of c.1840 with a long main street and long burgage plots lying perpendicular to it on either side. At the west end was the church and quite possibly a manor house as well as a market place, while to the east was the harbour which, by the 14th century, had acquired a pier and was a port of embarkation for troops bound for Ireland. With the church and manorial centre safely inland, the harbour end of Ilfracombe was probably originally a seasonal (?) fishing community (a fishing cellar) with its own chapel dedicated to St Nicholas, a saint favoured by mariners and fishermen. The strategic location of the safe harbour however, meant that it became increasingly important to shipping, so that in 1795 Ilfracombe was required to supply 49 ships to go to war against Napoleon. This growth in importance probably meant that the original borough area became neglected , descending into what a 17th century observer called 'one street lying scatteringly'.

Ilfracombe prides itself on being a Victorian town, and certainly large numbers of public and private buildings date from the Victorian era, but it is not the whole picture. Significant pre-Victorian buildings in the harbour area are the George and Dragon Inn, claiming to date from 1360, the manor house built by the Bourchier Wreys in the 1720s and the Britannia Hotel dating from the beginning of the 19th century. Elsewhere – near the parish church, along and behind the High Street and in the Fore Street area.-. there are odd surviving vernacular buildings that are worth seeking out. However, the now familiar character of Ilfracombe has it roots in the late Georgian and Regency period when Ilfracombe became 'much frequented' on account

Ilfracombe in 1840, view towards Hillsborough with the Wilder Brook in the valley and Adelaide Terrace, one of the first of the late Georgian terraces visible in the far distance. (Ilfracombe Museum)

of its 'salubrious air and waters'. In the 1820s two beaches were made accessible by the digging of tunnels through the cliff, and in 1836 the Bath House was built in the classical Grecian style for those who found the sea too bracing. It was the decade of the 1830s that saw the beginnning of building on a grand scale with Hillsborough, Montpelier and Adelaide Terraces built in classical Georgian style to provide town houses by the sea for wealthy families. From the 1830s onwards classical styles of building gave way to the Gothic Revival. A precursor of this development was Runnymede House, built near the Bath House, but unlike the Bath House designed in the late 18th century style attributed to Horace Walpole and known as Strawberry Hill Gothic. Castle House, Hillsborough Road is similarly built. Other buildings exemplify the transformation of Ilfracombe during the period 1830 to 1860, but it was in the 1860s that Victorian Ilfracombe blossomed due to the efforts of a group of entrepreneurs who resolved to make Ilfracombe the Brighton of the South West. The striking buildings of this period, designed in a profusion of variations on the neo-Gothic style, are too numerous to list here: it is well worth acquiring a copy of 'The Buildings of ilfracombe' by Jim Bates (2005) and walking round the town with this in hand. (See the entry' Resorts' for further information).

Among the smaller towns of Northern Devon, South Molton and Great Torrington display the most prominent marks of past prosperity. Both were turned into boroughs in the 12th/13th century period, the characteristic lay-out of which is clearly visible in South Molton, somewhat less so in Torrington. Great Torrington was already a valuable and populous manor at the time of the Domesday survey, and when it became a borough was evidently a significant market, being known as Chipping Torrington (*chipping* means 'market'). In the 13th century a castle was built here overlooking the valley of the Torridge, but having been built without permission from the Crown was ordered to be torn down in 1228. The best remembered event in Torrington's history is the Civil War battle of 1646 when Fairfax defeated the Royalists who had taken the town. As with other small Devonshire towns, prosperity was derived from the wool trade and, in Torrington's case, from tanning and the production of leather goods, especially gloves. Similarly the prosperity of the medieval borough of South Molton derived from cattle and wool.

Of the other towns mentioned at the beginning of this entry, Holsworthy, Hatherleigh and Hartland (as Harton) were medieval boroughs, but Northam was not. In 1086, Harton and Holsworthy were held by the King, while Tavistock Abbey held Hatherleigh. Northam was held by St Stephen's church of Caen to which it had been granted by Queen Matilda. It was a valuable possession having land for 20 ploughs, 23 villagers, two salt-houses and a fishery paying 30 pence. The manor was valued at £12. It is thought probable that the fishery was at Appledore, which may have been the 'fishing cellar' of the manor of Northam.

Northam exemplifies a class of over-large villages, some of

which have become officially towns. Among those that have not reached this status are Combe Martin, Braunton, Winkleigh, Chulmleigh, North Molton and Bradworthy. Among these only Braunton was never a borough and never had a market charter. If we take the others together with the towns discussed above (apart from Ilfracombe), we can begin to recognise what it is or was that makes them significant, namely that they provide market places that are roughly a day's journey apart in the days of horse-drawn transport: they are, in the geographer's terms, 'central places'. (TG)

Further Reading

Bates J 2005: *The Buildings of Ilfracombe*, Ilfracombe

Beresford M and Finberg H P R 1973: *English Medieval Boroughs: A Handlist*, Newton Abbot.

Cherry B and Pevsner N 2002: *The Buildings of England: Devon*, Yale

Grant A & Christie P 2005: *The Book of Bideford: The Development of a Devonian Market Town*, Wellington.

Hoskins W G 1954 (and later editions): *Devon*, Tiverton

Lamplugh L 2002: *Barnstaple: Town on the Taw*, Chichester

Underwater Archaeology

While the coast of South Devon has seen quite considerable underwater archaeological investigation by divers, the Northern Devon coast presents a more challenging environment restricting the opportunities for discovery. The well known surfing beaches of North Devon represent the very reason why marine archaeological investigation has been limited: The high surge environment which prevails most of the year, reduces visibility, demolishes wrecks quickly and makes for a short diving season. The potential however, is great: The mouth of the Taw/Torridge estuary is a danger for shipping despite beckoning as a shelter. This is due to the infamous bar across the estuary mouth and the tidal race (warned against in the 19th century Bristol Channel Pilot). There were over 50 recorded losses here in the 18th and 19th centuries alone. Who knows what earlier vessels may be buried there? Discovery is at present unlikely however as this area would be a high risk dive environment. In many ways the most intriguing aspect of underwater archaeology in Northern Devon is what has not been found. The number of wrecks on Bideford bar has already been mentioned but perhaps the greatest potential lies in the anaerobic intertidal silts of the estuary. Perhaps somewhere there lies a sewn plank Bronze Age boat similar to those found further up the Severn estuary. Or an Iron Age dug out canoe? Certainly the silt would ensure good preservation and such finds would be of national importance.

Apart from the well known Mesolithic midden site in the intertidal zone at Westward Ho! and accumulations of pottery in the river silts, the conditions outlined here mean that, for the most part, the region's underwater and marine archaeology is represented by wrecks and hulks of the 18th -20th centuries, most of which are accessible only to trained divers.

There are however, a number of wrecks which are intertidal (and therefore accessible) but still come under the auspices of marine archaeology. There is an unidentified wreck at Saunton Sands marked on a chart of 1851 which is at present sanded (approx. SS440 353). There are also records of three other wrecks further up the beach to the north. On the other side of the estuary is another beached wreck, this time generally visible at low tide (SS431 298). It is now thought (thanks to dendrochronology) to be the Sally, an 18th century vessel wrecked due to positional error in fog. All the crew escaped. Some 250 metres from the Sally is another wreck, often uncovered at low tide (SS432 300). The dimensions correspond with those of a Polacca Brig, a vessel used in the limestone trade (servicing the many limekilns visible along the coast and estuary).

Diving off Lundy: The boilers of the Iona. (James Wright)

Also accessible on foot at low tide are a number of hulks in the estuary. These are vessels deliberately beached or abandoned. There are too many to detail here (several books/articles can be sourced for more information), but a few can be highlighted. From the road between Westward Ho! and Appledore can be seen a long keelson outlined in the mud (SS457 308). This is all that remains of the schooner Goldseeker, of interest as it was once owned by the notorious Blackshirt Oswald Mosely. Nearby, (SS456 308) are the sparse remains of a Thames barge, a long way from home. In a little cove easily accessed from the footpath between Bideford and Appledore are the remains of four vessels, all of which have deteriorated significantly in the last few decades (SS462 289). The best preserved is the MA James, a topsail schooner built for trade with Newfoundland and bought by Captain Slade of Bideford in 1930. The others, ketches, were all built in the West Country and locally owned.

Further towards Appledore on the foreshore near Appledore Shipbuilders are more hulks (SS466 297). Access is problematic at present, but they can at least be viewed from the footpath. Two of these have connections to well known local families. One, Ketch (a rather unimaginative name for a ketch) was brought to

Appledore by the Jewell family in the 1920s. Further towards the channel is the Margaret Hobley, a schooner. This was another vessel owned by the Slade family who later wrote about their experiences in the classic 'Out of Appledore'.

As for deep water remains, Lundy Island is exceptional in the region, presenting more favourable conditions both for diving and for the preservation of remains. Given its position in the Bristol Channel, Lundy is a 'ship trap'.Here, off the more sheltered east side of the island, are two wrecks of national importance, both of which are designated (ie. protected). The first, the Gull Rock wreck is enigmatic. There is little visible: a few cannon and some stone shot suggest an approximate 14th to 15th century date. Present policy tends towards mothballing such sites, but there may be further evidence beneath the silts when excavation does take place in the future.

The second wreck, the Iona II, is remarkable in many ways. A paddle steamer of innovative design (for 1863) it was nearly 75 metres in length and built in Govan for coastal work. Shortly afterwards however, it was bought by a Virginian, allegedly for blockade running in the American Civil War. It was stripped of passenger fittings and loaded with coal for the Atlantic voyage. This cargo, its flat bottom and shallow draught, meant the journey was barely begun before the vessel fetched up on the rocks at Lundy and sank. It was designated in 1989 due to its unique engine and intact engineering, including boilers (see photo).

The coast around Hartland Point has always presented dangers to shipping and was notoriously the abode of wreckers. Quite aside from criminal acts, the shore from Hartland Point to Hartland Quay and beyond has probably for centuries seen ships driven by storm and tide to their deaths on the vicious rocks. The last remains of some of these can be seen on the shoreline as you walk the Coast Path, but the best way to learn more is to visit the Hartland Quay Museum where there is a collection of photographs and information. (CP)

Further Reading:
Milne S 1991: 'Incredible Hulks!' in *North Devon Heritage;* the Journal of the North Devon Museum Trust 3, 18-20
Slade W 1972: *Out of Appledore* (London)

Vikings

Seaborne warriors from Scandinavia –known in Old Norse as *Vikingar* 'adventurers'-began to lead raids on the British Isles and the coasts of western Europe in the late 8th century. Their activities continued into the 11th century, by which time the Norsemen and Danes had between them established a kingdom based on Dublin, settled half of England, placed a king on the English throne (Knut or Canute) and had dominated a large part of northern France, now known as Normandy. For seafaring warriors, especially those issuing out of Ireland, the long coastline of Devon and Cornwall was an obvious target, while the Bristol Channel offered direct access to the Kingdoms of Mercia and Wessex. Thus the Vikings' contribution to this account of Northern Devon's archaeology is a story of coastal assaults and the efforts to fend them off.

The earliest recorded such encounter dates from 836, when King Egbert of Wessex fought a large Viking force at Carhampton in north Somerset and lost. Thirty years later a 'great army' of Norsemen led by Ivarr and Halfdan began ten years of raiding throughout northern and central England, and in 875 a part of the army under Guthrum attacked King Alfred's Wessex. Alfred fended them off and Guthrum retreated to spend the winter at Gloucester. However, on Twelfth Night, Guthrum's army moved out of Gloucester to lead a surprise attack against Alfred who was at Chippenham. Alfred fled into the depths of Somerset where he famously took refuge at Athelney. Meanwhile a brother of Ivarr and Halfdan whose name was apparently Ubbe or Hubba was wintering in South Wales, from where he led a fleet of ships across the Bristol Channel to land on the coast of north Devon and lead an attack on Wessex from the west.

The story of Hubba the Dane and the battle of *Arx Cynuit* ('fort of Cynuit') has exercised many minds over the years. The story is briefly that Odda, the alderman of Devon, learning of the coming attack, gathered the King's thegns and their followers together in a fortified high place which was, according to King Alfred's biographer Asser, 'very secure from every direction except the east'. The Danes apparently knew that the place had no water, and so settled down to besiege it until the occupants had to leave. However, the men of Devon within burst out at dawn and overwhelmed the Vikings, killing 1200 of them including their leader Ubbe or Hubba. The remaining Vikings are said to have buried their leader by the shore.

The location of 'Cynuit' has been debated at length. There is a strong case for placing it at Wind Hill, an Iron Age promontory fort at Countisbury. There is also a supposition that it is at the mound called Kenwith Castle near Abbotsham, though this may be pure 19th century romantic fantasy. Recent private research has suggested that the site is that of Castle Hill, a hilltop enclosure in a bend of the Torridge south of Great Torrington (SS824 168). At Northam there is the tradition that the battle was fought at what is known as Bloody Corner and that Hubba was buried nearby. The question of what really happened remains unresolved.

Other lasting memorials of Viking attentions to Northern Devon are the name of Lundy, which is from Old Norse *lund-eg*, meaning 'puffin island' (like other islands in the Bristol Channel, Lundy would have had strategic use) and the origins of Barnstaple as a borough. After defeating the Danes at the battle of Edington (Wiltshire) in 878, King Alfred decreed the setting up of a number of fortified towns or 'burhs' across the south of England as a permanent means of defence against the Danes. These are recorded in a document known as the Burghal Hidage. Four of the southwestern *burhs* were to be in Devon at Exeter,

Halwell (later Totnes), Lydford and Pilton. There is a question about the identity or location of the *burh* of Pilton, but whatever was meant by it, the fortified *burh* that emerged from Alfred's policy was Barnstaple. (TG)

Further Reading:

Gore D 2001: *The Vikings and Devon*, The Mint Press, Exeter.

Weirs, fish

The term fish-weir is used to describe what are perhaps more accurately called fish traps (also called 'kiddles') which are still in use in many parts of the world. They comprise a series of stakes and accompanying wood and wickerwork strung out into the main channels of a tidal river with the aim of driving fish into traps. Most, but not all were of a V-shape with the trap itself at the junction of the two wings. Only the stumps of the main stakes have survived and some fish weirs known in the mid-19th century from documents and maritime charts have been completely engulfed by silt and sand and may only rarely be

The remaining stakes of a fish weir on the foreshore at Ashford Strand

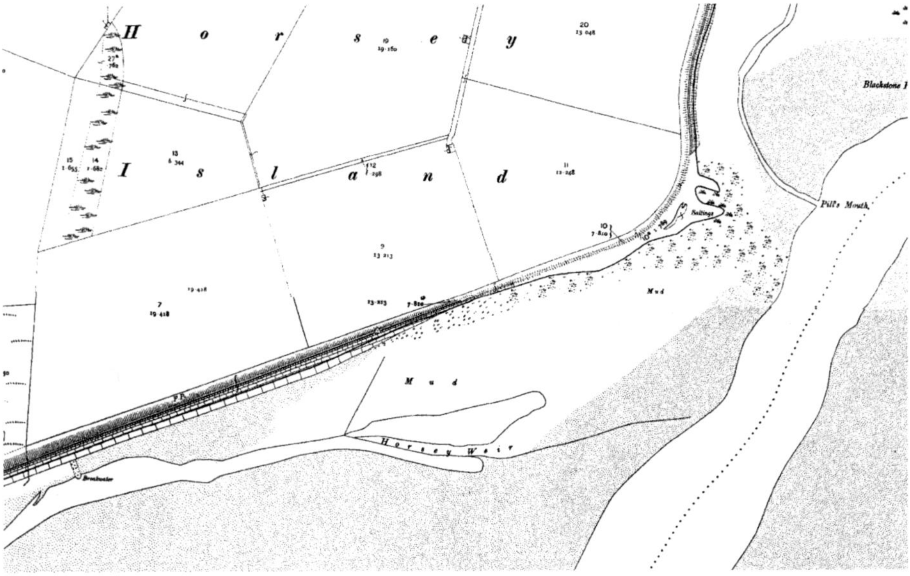

The Horsey Island Fish weir as recorded in 1905.

glimpsed. It is also important to remember that not all stakes and posts now visible in the inter-tidal mud were once fish weirs. Some were mooring posts and others, especially along the stretch from Westleigh Strand to Instow were installed for gang-ways to link the many ships laid up here in the 1920s and 1930s to the shore. Some stakes in tidal creeks like the river Yeo at Landcross were intended to aid navigation. A North Devon Archaeological Society project from 1999-2008 discovered 18 fish weirs in the Taw estuary known from charts and maps from the first half of the nineteenth century. At least four weirs were located near Crow Point, principally to the west of the present sand spit and another was located on the south side of Horsey Island. Remains of this quite enormous structure are occasionally revealed by shifting sand and the outline is clearly shown on the 1:25 000 OS map at (SS478 333). Another weir that is fairly easy to find is that at Ashford Strand, close to the lime kiln (SS523 348). Fish weirs are almost impossible to date. They were constantly rebuilt, often re-using stakes from older structures. The earliest documentary indication we have is a 9th century charter granting Brannocmynster or Braunton to Glastonbury Abbey 'for the taking of fish.' Domesday Book records fisheries at Bideford, Braunton, Heanton and Weare Giffard, but whether these were fish weirs or a net fishery is not known, although at this time the larger fisheries tended to be fish weirs. There was a potential conflict between fish weirs and navigation, as recognised in Magna Carta one of whose clauses demanded the removal of fishweirs from rivers throughout England, though the coast was excepted. Several times in the 19th century men from Appledore tried to destroy the weirs at Crow Point. The 1861 Salmon Fisheries Act curbed the use of fish weirs and many of those in the Taw and Torridge went out of use at this time. A few survived into the twentieth century and then attracted the same opprobrium as the boat and net salmon fishery in the estuary for taking too many fish to the detriment of the salmon fly fishery on the fresh water up-stream. Henry Williamson in the 1930s in his *Tales of Estuary and Moorland* nicely captures what amounts to the class antagonism of the fishermen of Appledore to the gentlemen fly-fishermen upstream. (JB)

Further reading:

Preece C (2008) *A Field Guide to the Archaeology of the Taw and Torridge Estuaries*. Bideford: Edward Gaskell.

World War 2

Although relating to only seventy years ago, the archaeology of the Second World War in Northern Devon is often quite subtle. During 1940 with the threat of invasion very real, beaches were protected by concrete and barbed wire defences. Almost all of these were removed very quickly and there remain a few concrete bases such as those by the southern end of Marine Parade in Instow (SS473 302). At the same time, on the other side of the Torridge estuary between Bideford and Appledore a

set of 'dragon's teeth', an anti-tank device, remains in place on the footpath at SS486 285.

Dragon's teeth on the footpath from Bideford to Appledore.

As part of the national air-defence network a radar station was constructed on Northam Burrows, one of the transmitter buildings surviving off Burrows Lane (SS453 304), looking more like a large air-raid shelter. A little to the west, the concrete foundations for the steel tensioning wires of the transmitter aerials, now long gone, can also be found. Perhaps the major piece of World War 2 construction in Northern Devon was RAF Winkleigh constructed from 1940-43. The plateau just north of Winkleigh village was flat and of low agricultural value but proved to be extremely wet and a major challenge to the engineers. Two run-ways were laid out, one running NNW-SSW and the other at right angles to it. This latter survives and can be seen from the A3124 which crosses the airfield site. The

A dummy pillbox on Baggy Point.

control tower is also visible to the NE from the road. The airfield (SS61-09, 62-09 and 62-08) was used for a variety of aviation missions, especially in the period leading up to the D-Day landings. It closed in 1948 but was briefly re-activated in 1956 during the Suez crisis. It was finally disposed of in 1958 and has been subsequently used for a variety of industrial and commercial purposes.

Of especial interest, because physical remnants are still visible in the landscape, is the US Assault Training Centre based at Croyde. This was a unique establishment of World War II, created through necessity by the U.S. Army to train their troops who would spearhead the D-Day landings in Normandy.

The area set aside was all land west of a line approximately from Ilfracombe to the Taw and Torridge estuary including beaches at Saunton, Croyde and Woolacombe, Baggy Point and Braunton Burrows.

Between September 1943 and March 1944 over ten thousand American soldiers practised the deadly arts and tactics of amphibious assault in three-week training courses.

Because of the topography of the beaches that the Americans were to assault on D-Day, tanks and armoured vehicles could not be used, so neutralising enemy bunkers and strongholds had to be done by the infantry. This involved new skills in the use of explosives and tactics and the very reason the Assault Training Centre was created.

The principle adopted was based upon a thirty man "Assault section". Each was a self-contained team of specialists capable of destroying an enemy pillbox. Riflemen, machine guns and mortars to return fire to the enemy, Bazooka rockets to fire at the pillbox alongside flamethrowers, Bangalore torpedoes to blow open barbed wire defences and finally demolition men carrying large explosives rushed the pillbox to neutralise it.

Trainees were acclimatised to sea voyages in small landing craft launched at Crow Point, introduced to new weapons and constantly drilled using live ammunition under battle conditions on ranges on Braunton Burrows. Full scale beach assaults with smoke, explosions and artillery fire were conducted at Woolacombe to round off each training course.

Few American constructions survived the post war demolition training of the British army on Braunton Burrows, but Baggy Point still has several dummy pillboxes intact and the lower reaches of Saunton Sands have concrete structures in the dune line. Shifting sands in the winter can also reveal remnants of metal work and concrete between high and low water marks.

Research and exploration has located many structures on Braunton Burrows, the remainder having been reclaimed by nature and covered by blown sand or vegetation. But there are personal mementos still to be seen. On Baggy Point a soldier of the 146th Engineer Combat Battalion who were responsible for the construction and maintenance of training aids wrote his name in the wet concrete during construction. He was Private Alfred A. Augustine who was killed in action on Omaha beach on D-Day. At the rear of a dummy landing craft the 1st platoon, Company C of the 146th Engineers left their mark and suffered grievous casualties on Omaha beach on D-Day.

Almost a quarter of the ten thousand soldiers who came here

to learn the arts of war became casualties on the Normandy beaches in one day, yet the Commandant, Colonel Paul W. Thompson said 'If Waterloo was won on the playing fields of Eton, surely the sands of the North Devon beaches contributed importantly to the success of the assault over the Normandy beaches'. (RB)

Further Reading:
Bass R T 1994: *Spirits of the Sand: The History of the US Assault Training Centre, Woolacombe*, Lee Publishing, Exeter.
Ace Archaeoolgy Club (1999, 2008) *Winkleigh Airfield*: A Survey. www.achearch.org.uk/acreports/AirfieldSurvey.pdf (Accessed 12.09.2013)

Yeo and other River Names:

Rivers are very significant features and reference points in the landscape acquiring names in the course of time which are in a class of their own as opposed to the names of settlements. The majority of Devon's rivers retain their Brittonic (Celtic) name. In our area Taw derives from a Brittonic term meaning ' the silent one', while Torridge is 'the turbulent one', the Tamar, recorded bythe Greek geographer Ptolemy in the first century AD, has a name related to Thames as well as Tavy and appears to mean something like 'flowing'. The various smaller rivers called Yeo, on the other hand – and they are quite numerous – acquire their names from Old English. 'Yeo' means simply 'water' and hence 'stream'. This is rather like the various Avons whose names are Brittonic in origin, meaning simply 'river'; similarly Exe and Axe also mean 'water'.

Dull as the name Yeo appears to be, it may be of interest to trace some of its more exotic relationships. The name derives from Old English *ēa* which features in river-based place-names throughout England. The word, meaning water or stream, was pronounced 'ay-ah' normally with stress on the 'ay', but in the

Southwest the stress shifted to the 'ah' so that it sounded like 'yah'. With lip-rounding, this developed into 'yo', spelt Yeo. In earliest Old English the word was ah, the *'h'* representing a sound like Scottish loCH. Descending ultimately, via Common Germanic *ahwa*, from an ancestral Indo-European word for water *akwa*, its relatives appear as the *-ach* on the end of a number of German river-names (Biberach, Salzach, Goldach, etc), the Latin word *aqua* 'water', and even the *-ab* in India's Punjab, 'the land of the five waters'. So between the Devonshire Yeos and the waters of north India, there is a common linguistic heritage. The name Yeo is more interesting than at first appears.

Some of our river names are so-called 'back-formations', which means that any original name has been lost and a name has been created deriving from that of a major settlement on the river. Thus the Mole is named from Molton, the Claw is named from Clawton, the Mere probably from Merton and the Bray from High Bray. Purely English names are few but include Lyn from Old English *hlynn* 'torrent' and Pill (an earlier nameof the Yeo as it flows by Pilton) from Old English *pyll* ' tidal creek'. Further Brittonic names on the fringes of our chosen area are the (Little) Dart, 'oak river' and the Okement, 'sluggish, slow flowing'. (TG)

Further Reading:

Gover J, Mawer A and Stenton F 1931: *The Place-names of Devon*, Part 1, Cambridge

Yews

Yew trees are a well known feature of British churchyards, the reason for which lends itself to a great deal of speculation. In 1307 Edward I issued a decree that yews should be planted in churchyards in order to protect the building from high winds and storms, so at least a proportion of our churchyard yews were planted for practical reasons (though there has to be doubt about

The multi-stemmed trunk of one of Shirwell's ancient yews.

their effectiveness). In Ireland yews were planted in or around churchyards from the eighth century. However, nationally there are indications that some ancient yew trees pre-date the churches by which they stand. Certainly their longevity and their evergreen foliage are suggestive of the preservation and continuity of life and it is quite possible to believe that the yew tree had mythic or ritual significance in pre-Christian Britain. It is also possible to believe that early Christian missionaries deliberately adopted sites marked by yew trees in order to claim them for Christ.

In our area yews are commonly found in churchyards, some of them relatively young, others evidently ancient. The photograph here shows one of a pair of yews in the churchyard of St Peter's Church in Shirwell. In the Exeter Diocese list of Devonshire churchyard yews these are classified as 'veteran', while the church history that you can pick up inside the church states that their age has been scientifically determined at 1,500 years, which would make them 'ancient'. If this is the case then they suggest a very early origin for this Christian site. Its location in an elevated position might suggest an ancient meeting place, and in fact among the names of the 'hundreds' of Devon, Shirwell Hundred is one of very few named after a significant topographic feature (Anglo-Saxon *scierewielle* 'clear spring') as opposed to a significant settlement (Braunton, Fremington, Hartland et al.) The name may refer to the water that issues from the ground not far below the eminence on which the church stands. In other parts of the country hundreds are commonly named after meeting places marked by natural features, so the ancient yews of Shirwell may well carry this kind of association.

One further matter of interest (and relevant since this is the last alphabetic entry in our catalogue) is that 'yew' is the name of the fifth letter of the ancient Irish ogham alphabet and the thirteenth letter of the runic alphabet. (TG)

Further Reading:
Friar S 1996: *A Companion to the English Parish Church*, Sutton Publishing, Stroud.
Mac Coitir N 2003: *Irish Trees: Myths, Legends and Folklore,* Collins Press, Cork.

Appendix A

Chronology

Archaeologists and historians have divided the past up into periods and we shall use the rough chronology set out in Table 1. The Palaeolithic (Old Stone Age) covers a vast period of time and includes the first known human activity in Britain, the recently discovered flint tools and human footprints at Happisburgh in Norfolk, thought to date from 850,000 to 950,000 years ago. The earliest human remains found in Devon are those from Kent's Cavern in Torquay, which are now dated to around 41,500 to 44,000 years ago and are thus older than the 'Red Lady of Paviland' (actually a man) from the Gower coast across the Bristol Channel, dated to c 33,000 years ago. Approximate dates for succeeding periods are displayed in the table below.

Table 1

Period	Dates
Palaeolithic	1 million years to 12,000 years ago
Mesolithic	12,000 to 6,500 years ago (10,000 to 4,500 BC)
Neolithic	6,500 to 4,500 years ago (4,500 to 2,500 BC)
Bronze Age	4,500 to 2,700 years ago (2,500 to 700 BC)
Iron Age	2,700 to 1,950 years ago (700 BC to AD 50)
Romano-British	1,950 to 1,540 years ago (AD 50 to AD 410)
Post-Roman	1,540 to 1,300 years ago (AD 410 to AD 700)
Early Medieval	1,300 to 900 years ago (AD 700 to AD 1100)
Late Medieval	500 to 900 years ago (AD 1100 to AD 1500)
Early Modern	250-500 years ago (AD 1500 to AD 1750)
Modern	70- 250 years ago (AD 1750 to AD 1940)
Contemporary	0-70 years ago (AD 1940 to date)

Fuller coverage of the prehistoric and medieval periods is to be found in the alphabetically ordered text.

The record of humans in Northern Devon starts in the Mesolithic (Middle Stone Age) typically with the midden site at Westward Ho! although, in fact, evidence of a Mesolithic presence, mainly in the form of flint scatters, is widespread both along the coast and inland. By the Neolithic (New Stone Age), there is, nationally, more substantial evidence of human activity. Scatters of flints and debris from flint working characteristic of the Neolithic are found across most of Northern Devon, while on Exmoor standing stones and stone rows are probably from this period. Northern Devon has far more substantial evidence of human activity in the Bronze Age and the Iron Age, the latter rather arbitrarily concluded at AD 43, when the Romans invaded and stayed. While the British tribal territory of the Dumnonii (Devon, Cornwall and West Somerset) came under Roman control after roughly AD 50, Northern Devon is something of an enigma in the Roman period, with odd finds of Roman coins, some scraps of pottery and a few first century military sites. There is evidence of considerable Romano-British iron working in the Bray valley but very little else to suggest more than three centuries within the Roman Empire. Following the collapse of Roman administration – traditionally set at AD 410 - the post-Roman polity of Dumnonia enjoyed more or less three centuries of independence before being progressively incorporated into Anglo-Saxon Wessex from the late seventh century.

The whole period from the fifth century until around the Norman Conquest in 1066 is usually described as Early Medieval. Of this formative period very little artefactual evidence remains, yet it is in this period that almost all of the settlements that we recognise in the Northern Devon landscape today came into being. In the later Medieval period c 1100 to c 1550 settlement development progressed and the landscape took more of the shape that we recognise, so that by the end of the period, almost all of what we see today was in existence.

The period from 1500 to c 1750 can be regarded as another

distinct phase. During this period Northern Devon joined in the opening up of trade across the Atlantic, while much of its religious and political character was formed during and in the aftermath of the English Civil Wars of the mid 17th century. The agricultural and industrial revolutions of the 18th century were felt in Northern Devon and c 1750 may be regarded as the start of the modern period. Perhaps, so that Word War 2 sites can be included, it might be appropriate to call 1940 the start of the contemporary period, or is it just that two of the authors were born in the decade 1940-1949?

A note on dating:
Traditionally the years before the birth of Christ are referred to as 'BC' (Before Christ) and those after as 'AD' (Anno Domini, Latin for 'in the year of our Lord'). It is an increasingly common practice in a multicultural world to refer to the earlier period as 'BCE' (Before Common Era), though 'AD' remains in in use beside CE. Radio-carbon dates are quoted as 'BP', that is 'Before Present', where the 'Present' is 1950, after which date the effects of Cold War nuclear testing have the potential to compromise radio-carbon dates which are based on the nuclear decay of carbon isotope Carbon 14.

Further reading:
Grinsell, LV (1970) *The Archaeology of Exmoor: Bideford Bay to Bridgwater.* Newton Abbot: David and Charles.
Riley, H & Wilson-North, R (2001) *The Field Archaeology of Exmoor.* Swindon: English Heritage.

Appendix B

How to Read a National Grid Reference (NGR)

In this small volume we have provided examples of sites which are accessible to the public either on common or access land or by viewing from a public footpath. We have located these sites with a National Grid Reference. The following explanation is intended to guide those who are unfamiliar with the grid reference system.

1. The preferred map is the Ordnance Survey Explorer Series at a scale of 1:25 000 (that is 4 centimetres to one kilometre).

2. Explorer maps numbers 126, 127, 139 and parts of 114 and OL9 (Exmoor) encompass the area covered by this A-Z.

3. The Ordnance Survey divides the whole country into 100km x 100km squares which are identified by letters. Our area falls largely within square SS, with a small area.in square SX. Thus any grid references in this area are prefixed with the letters SS, unless given SX.

4. The map itself is divided into 1km squares which are numbered south-north (northings) and west-east (eastings).

5. Between the numbers there are divisions each representing one tenth of a kilometre.

6. A typical NGR might be SS333 211. This is a six-figure grid reference which for our purposes is precise enough. You read this by looking along the eastings to 33.3 and up the northings to 21.1. Where the two meet is your location. The easy way to remember is to say 'along the passage and up the stairs'. If you've followed this on the map you should have found the church in Woolfardisworthy.

7. In some cases we have given a four figure grid reference. This is where the location in question is not a specific point, but a small area. In these cases the numbers will take you to a grid square within which you should find the feature.

Glossary of possibly unfamiliar terms

Anaerobic: From which air is excluded. Under anaerobic conditions organic matter may be preserved.

Ashlar: In architecture, stone which is dressed square

Brittonic: Pertaining to the native Britons in the period after the collapse of Roman administration.

Chronology: The arrangements of events in the order in which they occurred.

Crenellated: With a battlemented top, like a tower or castle.

Dendrochronology: Dating by tree-rings, which differ year by year depending on the weather.

Ecclesiastical: To do with the Church.

Feudal: The social order of the early Middle Ages, lords at the top , serfs at the bottom, the lower orders owing dues to thos above them.

Hornwork: A term used to describe the sometimes quite intricate arrangement of interlocking passages providing access to a hillfort.

Hundred: An administrative division above manors and parishes, thought to be originally an area of land that could raise a hundred fighting men.

Morphological: To do with shape or form.

Multivallate: Having more than one defensive bank or rampart.

Ovoid: roughly oval

Palladian: Pertaining to the 18th century architectural style based on Greek and Roman temple architecture.

Palaeoenvironmental: Pertaining to preserved ancient organic matter which provides evidence of past environments.

Reveals: In architecture, the edges of window openings.

Secular: Worldly, not to do with the Church.

Univallate: Having a single bank or rampart.

Vernacular: In architecture, pertaining to more humble, everyday buildings such as farmhouses and cottages.

Index of Places mentioned in the Text

Sources and References:

Ace Archaeoolgy Club (1999, 2008) Winkleigh Airfield: A Survey. www.achearch.org.uk/acreports/AirfieldSurvey.pdf

Allan J, Horner B, & Langman G, 2005: Seventeenth- and eighteenth-century pottery waste from the Stella Maris Convent School Site, Bideford, Proceedings of the Devon Archaeological Society 63.

Allan J, Cramp C, & Horner B, 2007: The post-medieval pottery at Castle Hill, Great Torrington, North Devon, Proceedings of the Devon Archaeological Society 68, 135-181.

Atkinson M (ed) 1997: Exmoor's Industrial Archaeology, Tiverton: Exmoor Books.

Aston M 1985: Interpreting the Landscape: Landscape Archaeology and History, London: Routlege.

Claughton P 2004: The Combe Martin Mines, 3rd edn, Combe Martin Local History Group.

Claughton P, Paynter S and Dunkerley, T 2005: Further work on lead smelting at Combe Martin, Devon, http://people.exeter.ac.uk/pfclaugh/mhinf/Lead_si.pdf

Curl J S (2006, 2nd edition) Oxford Dictionary of Architecture and Landscape Architecture. Oxford: Oxford University Press.

Barker P and Higham R 1994: Timber Castles, University of Exeter Press, Exeter.

Bass R T 1994: Spirits of the Sand: The History of the US Assault Training Centre, Woolacombe, Lee Publishing, Exeter.

Beacham P (ed) 1995: Devon Building: An Introduction to Local Traditions, Tiverton: Devon Books.

Beresford M and Finberg H P R 1973: English Medieval Boroughs: A Handlist, Newton Abbot: David and Charles.

Blanchard L. 1988: Archaeology in North Devon 1987-8. North Devon District Council Rescue Archaeology Unit.

Bodman M (2009) Tanning in Devon in the nineteenth century, in Transactions of the Devonshire Association. 141. 219-236.

Boyle V and Payne D (1952) Devon Harbours. London: Christopher Johnson.

Brunskill R W 1978: Illustrated Handbook of Vernacular Architecture, Faber and Faber, London.

Butler C 2005: Prehistoric Flintwork, Stroud, Tempus.

Campbell S et al (eds.) 1998: Geological Conservation Review Series: Quaternary of South-West England, London.

Cherry B and Pevsner N 2002: The Buildings of England: Devon, Yale University Press

Claughton P 2004 The Combe Martin Mines, 3rd edn, Combe Martin Local History Group

Claughton P, Paynter S and Dunkerley T 2005 Further work on lead smelting at Combe Martin, Devon, http://people.exeter.ac.uk/pfclaugh/mhinf/Lead_si.pdf.

Coulter J 1993: Ancient Chapels of North Devon, Barnstaple.

Creighton O and Higham R 2003: Medieval Castles, Shire Books.

Curl J S 2006 (2nd edition): Oxford Dictionary of Architecture and Landscape Architecture. Oxford: Oxford University Press.

Darby H C and Welldon Finn R (eds), 1967: The Domesday Geography of South-West England, Cambridge.

Durrance E M and Laming D J C (eds) 1982: The Geology of Devon, Exeter.

Finberg H P R 1969: The Open Field in Devon, in West Country Historical Studies, David and Charles, Newton Abbot.

Fox A 1996: Prehistoric Hillforts in Devon, Exeter, Devon Books.

Fox H 2012: Dartmoor's Alluring Uplands, Exeter University Press.

Gelling M 1988: Signposts to the Past: Place-Names and the History of England, Chichester.

Gelling M and Cole A 2000: The Landscape of Place-Names, Lincoln.

Gover J, Mawer A and Stenton F 1931: The Place-names of Devon, Part 1, Cambridge.

Grant A & Christie P 2005: The Book of Bideford: The Development of a Devonian Market Town, Wellington: Hallsgrove.

Grant A and Jemmett D 1985 Pipes and Pipemaking in North Devon, in Davey, P.J. (ed) The Archaeology of the Clay Tobacco Pipe, IX BAR 146.

Green T 2009: Excavation of a Hillslope Enclosure at Holworthy Farm, Parracombe displaying Bronze Age and Iron Age Activity, in Proceedings of the Devon Archaeological Society, No. 67.

Griffith F 1988: Devon's Past: An Aerial View, Exeter, Devon Books.

Grinsell L V 1970: The Archaeology of Exmoor: Bideford Bay to Bridgwater, David and Charles.

Harris H and Ellis M 1972: The Bude Canal. Newton Abbot: David and Charles.

Hegarty C and Wilson-North R 2014: The Archaeology of Hill Farming on Exmoor, English Heritage.

Higham R 2008: Making Anglo-Saxon Devon, Exeter, The Mint Press.

Hoskins W G (1972, 2nd edition) Devon. Newton Abbot: David and Charles

Hoskins W G 1992 edition: The Making of the English Landscape (with commentary by Christopher Taylor, Hodder and Stoughton, London.

Hughes B D (2006) Rolle Canal and the North Devon Limestone Trade. Bideford: Edward Gaskell.

Farr G (1976) Shipbuilding in North Devon. Maritime Monograph and Report 22. National Maritime Museum, Greenwich.

Finberg H P R 1969: The Open Field in Devon, in West Country Historical Studies, David and Charles, Newton Abbot.

Friar S 1996: A Companion to the English Parish Church, Sutton Publishing: Stroud.

Gray T 2011: Devon's Fifty Best Churches, Exeter, Mint Press.

Gray T 2013: The Art of the Devon Garden, Exeter, Mint Press.

Grant A 2005: North Devon Pottery, Appledore, Edward Gaskell Publishing.

Green T 2009: Excavation of a Hillslope Enclosure at Holworthy Farm, Parracombe displaying Bronze Age and Iron Age Activity, Proceedings of the Devon Archaeological Society 67.

Gore D 2001: The Vikings and Devon, Exeter. The Mint Press,

Grinsell L V 1990: Barrows in England and Wales, Shire Publications

Kain R J P & Prince, C 1985: The Tithe Surveys of England and Wales, Cambridge: Cambridge University Press

Keene P 1996: Classic Landforms of the North Devon Coast, Sheffield:

Lamplugh L 2002 edition: Barnstaple: Town on the Taw, Chichester: Phillimore.

Lauder R (2005 revised edition) Vanished Houses of North Devon. Devon Books, Tiverton.

Lowe M C 1990: The Turnpike Trusts in Devon and their roads, 1753-1889, Transactions of the Devonshire Association 122. 47-69.

Mac Coitir N 2003: Irish Trees: Myths, Legends and Folklore, Collins Press: Cork.

Marsden B M 1999: The Early Barrow Diggers, Tempus Publishing: Stroud.

Messenger M (2007) North Devon Clay: The Story of an Industry and Its Railways, Truro: Twelveheads Press.

Minchinton W 1977: Windmills of Devon, Exeter Industrial Archaeology Group, Exeter.

Miles T 1987: The Excavation of a Saxon Cemetery and Part of the Norman Castle at North Walk, Barnstaple, in Proceedings of the Devon Archaeological Society 44.

Mitchell V & Smith K 1995: Taunton to Barnstaple. Midhurst: Middleton Press.

Newberry J 2002: Inland Flint in Prehistoric Devon, in Proceedings of the Devon Archaeological Society, Vol.60.

Nicholas J and Reeve G 2010: The North Devon Line: The Southern Railway Route between Exeter and Ilfracombe, Clophill, Bedforshire: Irwell Press

Orme N 2013: The Church in Devon 400-1560, Exeter, Impress Books.

Orme N 2013: Medieval Holy Wells in Devon, in Transactions of the Devonshire Association, 145.

Pearce S 1981: The Archaeology of South West Britain, London.

Pearce S 2004: South-western Britain in the Early Middle Ages, Leicester University Press.

Preece C 2008: A Field Guide to the Archaeology of the Taw and Torridge Estuaries, Bideford.

Preece C and Thompson P 2009 A Cache of early Clay Pipes from Appledore, in Proceedings of the Devon Archaeological Society 67.

Pugsley S (ed) (1994) Devon Gardens: An Historical Survey. Stroud: Alan Sutton

Riley H and Wilson-North R 2001: The Field Archaeology of Exmoor, English Heritage.

Rippon S, Claughton P and Smart C 2009 Mining in a Medieval Landscape: the Royal Silver Mines of the Tamar Valley, University of Exeter Press, (particularly Chapter 2)

Rogers W H 1942: Barnstaple Turnpike Trust, Transactions of the Devonshire Association 74. 139-168

Rothwell P and Ternstrom, M (2008) The Lundy Granite Company: An Industrial Adventure. Appledore: Westwell.

Shorter A H 1950: Field Patterns in Brixham, Devon, in Transactions of the Devonshire Association 82, 271-280.

Strong H W (1889) Industries of North Devon. Newton Abbot: David and Charles

Taylor C 2000 edition: Fields in the English Landscape, Alan Sutton, Stroud.

Terry R 1989: The Barnstaple Clay Tobacco Pipe Factory (NDDC Rescue Archaeology Unit).

Thomas C 1994: And Shall these Mute Stones Speak? University of Wales Press.

Thomas D StJ 1960 (revised edition 1996): A Regional History of the Railways of Great Britain: Volume 1 The West Country. Newton Abbot: David and Charles.

Thorn C and F 1985: Domesday Book: Devon. (2 volumes). Chichester: Philimore

Thorpe J (ed) 1989: North Devon Watermills. North Devon Archaeological Society, Barnstaple.

Todd M 1987: The South-West to AD 1000, London.

Turner S 2006: Making a Christian Landscape, Exeter University Press

Turner S (ed) 2006: Medieval Devon and Cornwall: Shaping an Ancient Countryside, Macclesfield: Windgather Press.

University of the Third Age. 1994: Watermills in North Devon, Barnstaple.

Welldon Finn R 1973: Domesday Book: A Guide. Chichester: Philimore.

Whiting F D 1948: Bideford Bridge, Transactions of the Devonshire Association 80. 127-136